Penguin Critical Studies

Jude the Obscure

Cedric Watts is Professor of English at the University of Sussex. He is the author of: *Conrad's 'Heart of Darkness': A Critical and Contextual Discussion* (1977); *Cunninghame Graham: A Critical Biography* (with Laurence Davies, 1979); *A Preface to Conrad* (1982); *R. B. Cunninghame Graham* (1983); *The Deceptive Text: An Introduction to Covert Plots* (1984); *A Preface to Keats* (1985); *Hamlet* (1988); *Joseph Conrad: A Literary Life* (1989); *Literature and Money: Financial Myth and Literary Truth* (1990); and *Romeo and Juliet* (1991). He has edited: *Joseph Conrad's Letters to R. B. Cunninghame Graham* (1969); *The English Novel* (1976); *Selected Writings of Cunninghame Graham* (1981); Conrad's *Lord Jim* (with Robert Hampson, Penguin 1986); *'Typhoon' and Other Tales* (1986); *The Nigger of the 'Narcissus'* (Penguin 1988); and *'Heart of Darkness' and Other Tales* (1990). He has also written the Penguin Critical Studies on *Nostromo* and *Measure for Measure*.

Penguin Critical Studies
Advisory Editor: Bryan Loughrey

Thomas Hardy

Jude the Obscure

Cedric Watts

Penguin Books

PENGUIN BOOKS

Published by the Penguin Group
Penguin Books Ltd, 27 Wrights Lane, London W8 5TZ, England
Penguin Books USA Inc., 375 Hudson Street, New York, New York 10014, USA
Penguin Books Australia Ltd, Ringwood, Victoria, Australia
Penguin Books Canada Ltd, 10 Alcorn Avenue, Toronto, Ontario, Canada M4V 3B2
Penguin Books (NZ) Ltd, 182–190 Wairau Road, Auckland 10, New Zealand

Penguin Books Ltd, Registered Offices: Harmondsworth, Middlesex England

First published 1992
10 9 8 7 6 5 4 3 2 1

Printed in England by Clays Ltd, St Ives plc
Set in Monophoto 9/11 Times

To Mike Owen,
Hardy fan and hearty friend,
and to all present-day Judes and Sues.

Contents

Part 1   Preliminary Matter

1.1   Editorial Notes; Acknowledgements; an Invitation

For the reasons given in Section 4.1, all quotations from the book version of *Jude the Obscure* are taken from the first edition, published by Osgood, McIlvaine & Co., London, in 1895 (though bearing the printed date '1896').

In any quotation, a row of three points (. . .) indicates an ellipsis already present in the printed text, whereas a row of five points indicates an omission that I have made. All other emendations to quoted passages are enclosed in square brackets. With these exceptions, I have endeavoured to present all quoted material without correction or alteration.

I am grateful to Ronald Draper and Roger Ebbatson for wise advice; to the staff of Sussex University Library for patient assistance; to John Sweet for editorial care; and to Alan Sinfield for helping to check the proofs.

Any students, young or old, who have questions about this book or Hardy's novel are welcome to write to me. My address is: Arts Building, University of Sussex, Brighton BN1 9QN.

1.2   The Plan of This Book

Part 2 offers a short biographical account of Thomas Hardy, suggesting various autobiographical aspects of *Jude the Obscure*. Part 3 discusses the novel's cultural contexts. In Part 4, I look in closer detail at the work's contents, considering a range of obvious topics: title, topography, structure, themes, characterization. Part 5 summarizes a selection of critics' opinions and offers retrospective comments on the text in the light of them. If the first half of this book seems to deal with 'contexts' and the second with 'contents', this is mainly a conventional distinction which reflection properly erodes. A monograph imposes a linear, consecutive sequence on matters which present themselves to the mind less as sequences than as mobile, interlinked and interchanging clusters.

I have gladly worked within the publisher's limit of 55,000 words; but there is, obviously, much more to be said about Hardy's *Jude the Obscure*. What I hope to have emphasized is that this is a richly paradoxical novel: elegant and untidy, fierce and uncertain, regressive and progressive, harrowing and humorous. Repeated analyses have not yet smoothed its roughnesses, nor have theoretical developments made it less defiantly awkward to grasp. It's a live text still, with plenty of fight left in it; and since it was fighting for a kinder world, that's just as well.

Part 2 Biographical

2.1 Hardy's Early Years

'To your enquiry if *Jude the Obscure* is autobiographical, I have to answer that there is not a scrap of personal detail in it, having the least to do with his own life of all his books.'[1]

That is how Hardy instructed his second wife to reply to an inquirer in October 1913. You might think, therefore, that there could be no more futile beginning to this book on *Jude the Obscure* than a biographical survey. But Hardy's reply is characteristically defensive. Repeatedly, when replying to critics and commentators, he sought to distance himself from his novels, arguing that they offered 'impressions' rather than convictions, tentative imaginings rather than doctrines, and had the objectivity of art rather than the subjectivity of the confessional. In one sense he was obviously right. Every statement in a fictional work is, so long as we are aware that we are reading fiction, a statement in quotation marks: part of an imaginative territory whose relationship to the actual world is shifting and variable, now close, now remote, but never fully coinciding. In another sense, though, he was obviously wrong.

Jude the Obscure is the last, and fiercest, of his sequence of novels. It is variously realistic and expressionistic; ironic and elegiac; symbolic and carefully researched; graphic and pedantic; satiric and poignant; comic and pessimistic; understated and strident; Victorian and modernistic; nostalgic and iconoclastic; clumsy and adroit; benign and bitter; subtle and blatant; rationalist and anti-rationalist; tragic and absurd; theological and sceptical. Its raw ferocity and insistent ruthlessness mingle with its keen sensitivity, compassion and modes of comedy. It depicts a riven battleground of ideas, beliefs, traditions and prejudices; it is a wounded and wounding novel. In all its tensions and conflicts, which it both describes and enacts, it is more intimately (if obliquely) autobiographical than the entirety of the lengthy autobiography which Hardy published in the guise of a biography written by his second wife. That *Life of Thomas Hardy* often voices reserve, prudence, detachment, circumspection; the novel voices the passion, anguish, anger and division of the deeper self. Through the mask of fictional identities and narration, Hardy speaks more vitally and comprehensively. W. B. Yeats wrote: 'We make out of the quarrel with others, rhetoric, but out of the quarrel with ourselves, poetry.'[2] Out of the quarrels with others and with himself, Hardy made *Jude the Obscure*. And to understand those quarrels, there is no better beginning than a survey of his life.

Thomas Hardy was born on 2 June 1840 in a thatched cottage at Higher Bockhampton, a village about three miles from Dorchester in Dorset. His father was a mason employing bricklayers; sometimes business was bad, sometimes it prospered. He was a smallholder, too, growing vegetables and fattening a pig for slaughtering each autumn. (Already there are glimpses of Jude, the mason appalled by the necessity to slaughter his pig.) Hardy's mother was a former maidservant and cook who had known poverty but who retained a strong, resilient personality, furthering her ambitions through her son in a way that anticipated D. H. Lawrence's maternal upbringing. Thus, in the rural society of south-west England, Hardy was born into an artisan 'caste' which was in close everyday contact with the humbler workers. As he explained in 1927: 'Down to the middle of the last century, country villagers were divided into two distinct castes, one being the artisans, traders, "liviers" (owners of freeholds), and the manor house upper servants; the other the "work-folk", i.e. farm labourers . . . . . '[3]

Rural life had its traditions, pastimes and festivities, but also its poverty, squalor and hardship: not far from the Hardys' home, the 'Tolpuddle Martyrs' had been sentenced to transportation (six years before Hardy's birth) for their attempts to organize a trade union. Hardy saw both the harshness of the countryside and its consolations: the beauties of the natural cycle, and the pleasures of music, whether folk-music, carols or hymns. His parents were keenly musical, his father playing the violin, and in course of time Hardy himself became an adroit, energetic fiddler at village dances. He was also intensely moved by the hymns and rituals of the Church of England during the family's regular attendance at Stinsford Church. 'As a child,' he later recalled of himself, 'to be a parson had been his dream':[4] another anticipation of Jude's aspirations.

One of the glories of Victorian England was its establishment of a nationwide educational system. Hardy entered the local National School when it opened in 1848. His early reading included popular novels by Lord Lytton, poems by W. J. Mickle, and Bunyan's *Pilgrim's Progress*: walking home from school, he was so frightened by Bunyan's description of Apollyon 'that he hastily closed his book and went on his way trembling, thinking that Apollyon was going to spring out of a tree whose dark branches overhung the road'. His fears thus resembled those of the young Jude, who 'started homewards at a run, trying not to think of giants, Herne the Hunter, Apollyon lying in wait for Christian . . . . . '⁵ There were also three volumes given to Hardy by his mother. One of these was Dryden's translation of Virgil's works, which initiated his lifelong study of the classics; and another was Johnson's *Rasselas*, that stoically pessimistic novel which declares, in tones which might be those of the world-weary Jude: 'Human life is everywhere a state in which much is to be endured, and little to be enjoyed.'⁶ The third volume was a translation of J.-H. Bernardin de Saint-Pierre's *Paul et Virginie* and of Sophie Cottin's *Élisabeth, ou Les Exiles de Sibérie*. A wise man in the former tale offers this unintentionally ironic advice:

'My son! talents . . . . . cost dear; they are generally allied to exquisite sensibility, which renders their possessor miserable . . . . . He who, from the soil which he cultivates, draws forth one additional sheaf of corn, serves mankind more than he who presents them with a book.'⁷

Many years later, Hardy's Jude, disillusioned with Christminster, would feel that humble artisans serve mankind more than can the scholars within the cloisters. Furthermore, as Phillotson will note, the intense romance of Paul with Virginia provided a precedent (as did Shelley's *The Revolt of Islam*) for the relationship of Jude with Sue: 'They remind me of Laon and Cynthia. Also of Paul and Virginia a little.'⁸ Those literary lovers were virtually siblings and exceptionally dedicated to each other.

Hardy's next school, the British School at Dorchester, gave him a grounding in Latin and French, while providing practical exercises in mathematics and letter-writing of a kind appropriate to boys entering trades. After his years here, Hardy was articled to John Hicks, a local architect, to be instructed in architectural drawing and surveying; and he frequently made surveys and measurements of churches that were to be 'restored' or modernized to suit Victorian tastes. Again like Jude, who, as a monumental mason, provides Victorian Gothic refurbishments, Hardy experienced misgivings about such truncations of a heritage by innovation. Near the opening of the novel is a characteristically sardonic passage:

[T]he original church, hump-backed, wood-turreted, and quaintly hipped, had been taken down, and either cracked up into heaps of road-metal in the lane, or utilized as pig-sty walls, garden seats, guard-stones to fences, and rockeries in the flower-beds of the neighbourhood. In place of it a tall new building of German-Gothic design, unfamiliar to English eyes, had been erected on a new piece of ground by a certain obliterator of historic records who had run down from London and back in a day.⁹

A further connection between Hardy and Jude was that, while working for the architect, Hardy found time to pursue a study of Greek, concentrating on the Greek New Testament; and, if Jude was inspired by Phillotson to dream of the intellectual life of Oxford University, Hardy's friend Horace Moule (who had studied at both Oxford and Cambridge) imparted similar visions of the cultural riches of a university education. Hardy never enrolled at a university, and always retained some of that sense of deprivation which is so marked in Jude; although, like the fictional character, Hardy knew that much of his own learning was often deeper, and certainly more hardly acquired, than that of many undergraduates whose wealthy backgrounds had gained them easy access to the collegiate cloisters.

In April 1862 he went to London and was employed as a draughtsman by Arthur Blomfield, inspecting sites, preparing drawings, and studying sufficiently well to win two professional prizes; he also found time to visit theatres, operas, art galleries and exhibitions. During his early years in London he apparently became engaged to Eliza Nicholls, a lady's maid from Dorset (later recalled in the 'She, to Him' sequence of poems), though his affection for her dwindled after Eliza left London for Godstone and Findon. Meanwhile, his friend Horace Moule, who had contributed articles, reviews and poems to a variety of periodicals, encouraged him to consider part-time journalism; and in 1865 *Chambers's Journal* paid Hardy over three pounds for publication of his satirical essay, 'How I Built Myself a House'. He was also assiduously studying poetry (Wordsworth, Shelley and Swinburne being among his favourite writers) and experimenting with a variety of verse-forms and topics ranging from the philosophically melancholy to the anecdotally comic.

His ambition of taking a Cambridge degree followed by a country curacy perished in 1866, when he told his sister Mary: 'I find on adding up expenses and taking into consideration the time I should have to wait, that my notion is too far fetched to be worth entertaining any longer.'[10] On the other hand, during his time in London his health and morale declined, and in 1867 he returned home to Bockhampton, working part-time for Hicks. There he fell in love with his 16-year-old cousin Tryphena Sparks, a pupil-teacher at an elementary school, who later, after proceeding to the Stockwell College of the British and Foreign Bible Society, became headmistress of a girls' school at Plymouth. Lively, fun-loving and energetic, Tryphena (later commemorated in the poem 'Thoughts of Phena') evidently contributed some traits to the eventual characterization of Sue Bridehead. Again, as her career took her away from frequent contact with Hardy, this relationship seems to have faded gradually. Another link with *Jude the Obscure*, however, is that Tryphena stayed for a while at the home of her (and Hardy's) aunt Mary at Puddletown; and Mary's husband, John Antell, was a self-educated man who knew Greek, Latin and Hebrew, and who seems to have fretted at the confines of his daily work as a shoemaker. He was 'a man of the working class who found no adequate outlet for his native abilities in the social conditions then prevailing, and whose frustrated energies erupted in bitterness, alcoholism, and violence'. Michael Millgate, one of Hardy's biographers, speculates that 'John Antell's deeply divided and tragically driven personality was central . . . . . to the whole conception of *Jude the Obscure*.' The speculation may be hyperbolic, but a striking piece of evidence is that when Antell was dying, he had himself photographed standing, bowed and fierce, beside a chair which bears a placard inscribed with the bitter words '*Sic placet*': 'This is pleasing'. [11]

In 1870 Hardy's architectural duties took him to the hamlet of St Juliot in Cornwall, where the dilapidated church needed renovation. At the rectory he was greeted by the 29-year-old Emma Gifford, the rector's sister-in-law. Emma, with her golden hair and rosy cheeks, a spirited horse-rider, soon captivated Hardy, who ever afterwards associated her with the romantic Cornish landscape and rugged coastline; and, though Emma noted that he was short, unhandsome and older-looking than his age, she deemed him a clever, well-read and liberating companion. After a courtship extending over years, they married in September 1874 at a parish church in London. Emma's father, a solicitor, felt that his daughter had demeaned herself by marrying a 'churl' with a Dorsetshire accent. Their marriage was to be childless and, eventually, bitterly unhappy. Hardy said that, when he first knew Emma, she was an agnostic (it might be truer to say that she wore her religion lightly); later she became an Evangelical, and eventually was obsessively devout. Again, there are glimpses of *Jude the Obscure* here: Hardy's movement towards greater scepticism clashed with Emma's increasing piety, anticipating that discordant counterpoint of scepticism and piety in the relationship between Jude and Sue. Many years later, in such famous poems as 'Beeny Cliff' and 'The Voice' written after Emma's death, Hardy looked back with poignant melancholy on the bygone exhilaration of their early days in Cornwall.

2.2 Literary Career to *Jude the Obscure*

Economically, the gateway to marriage had been opened by Hardy's increasing success as a fiction-writer. Whereas at the census of 1871 he had stated his profession as 'architect's clerk', in the marriage register he entered the word 'Author'.[12]

In 1867–8 Hardy had written a novel, *The Poor Man and the Lady*, about a young architect of humble background who secretly marries a squire's daughter, the squire having opposed the match. Hardy later stated:

The story was, in fact, a sweeping dramatic satire of the squirearchy and nobility, London society, the vulgarity of the middle class, modern Christianity, church restoration, and political and domestic morals in general, the author's views, in fact, being obviously those of a young man with a passion for reforming the world – those of many a young man before and after him; the tendency of the writing being socialistic, not to say revolutionary . . . . . [13]

The novel was sent to the Macmillan firm, and Alexander Macmillan himself wrote to the author at some length to praise several features and to assail others, notably 'the wholesale blackening of a class'; and he included a report from the firm's reader, John Morley, who criticized the form while seeing much 'stuff and promise'. Both men met Hardy and discussed literary possibilities with him, notably magazine work; but they declined the novel. Next, the manuscript went to Chapman & Hall, where another reader, the poet George Meredith, warned the author that, if *The Poor Man and the Lady* were published, reviewers would be outraged by its satiric boldness; Hardy should either 'soften' it or write a different novel with a more complicated plot. After subsequent travels and a rejection from Smith, Elder & Co., *The Poor Man and the Lady* returned to Hardy; it was never published, and the manuscript did not survive; but parts of it were incorporated in subsequent works. (Its rural scenes were expanded for *Under the Greenwood Tree*; the initial plot-situation and a scene set in Rotten Row – a scene praised by John Morley – reappeared in *A Pair of Blue Eyes*; and its social indignation eventually found reinvigorated expression in *Jude*.)

Following Meredith's unfortunate advocacy of a novel with a complicated plot, Hardy produced *Desperate Remedies*, a lurid but suspenseful melodramatic story. Its over-ingenious plotting owed something to the example of Wilkie Collins's *Basil* and particularly his *The Woman in White*, which provided the motif of impersonation of one woman by another. *Desperate Remedies* was packed with materials which, by the standards of the day, were distinctly sensationalistic. These materials included: a startlingly explicit lesbian encounter (perhaps indebted to Coleridge's 'Christabel'), in which a wealthy woman embraces in bed a beautiful young maidservant; a concealed murder, or manslaughter, of an alcoholic wife by her husband; the husband's stratagem of persuading his mistress to masquerade as his wife; and the hero's last-minute rescue of the young heroine from her honeymoon-night with her villainous spouse – who happens to be not only the wife-killer previously mentioned but also the illegitimate son of the wealthy woman. Rejected by Macmillan as too sensational, the book was accepted by William Tinsley, though Tinsley required the author to pay him £75 as a security against possible losses and to remove a passage concerning the 'violation of a young lady . . . . . at an evening party'.[14] Submitted in revised form in December 1870, it was published (with the customary rapidity of those days) on 25 March 1871; its anonymity indicated Hardy's diffidence.

The reviews were variable but included high praise. The *Athenaeum* declared that though *Desperate Remedies* was unpleasant as story and often coarse in expression, it was undoubtedly 'very powerful', showed 'considerable artistic power', contained one character 'almost worthy of George Eliot', and displayed an assured use of West Country dialect. If the author could only purge himself of the coarseness, 'we see no reason why he should not write novels only a little, if at all, inferior to those of the best of the present generation.' The *Morning Post* offered praise. The *Spectator*'s review began ferociously:

This is an absolutely anonymous story; no falling back on previous works which might give a clue to the authorship, and no assumption of a *nom de plume* which might, at some future time, disgrace the family name, and still more, the Christian name of a repentant and remorseful novelist . . . . .

The author's powers, the review continued, had been 'prostituted to the purposes of the idle prying into the way of wickedness'; perhaps he had sought 'desperate remedies' for 'ennui or an emaciated purse'; in the wealthy lady he had depicted a character 'uninteresting, unnatural, and nasty'. Nevertheless, the reviewer praised the depiction of 'village rustics' (quoting lengthy illustrative passages) and noted shrewdly the author's 'sensitiveness to scenic and atmospheric effects'. (Hardy, reading this piece as he sat on a stile by a country road, wished himself dead.) A further appraisal, in the *Saturday Review*, was much more positive: not surprisingly, for it was written by Hardy's friend, Horace Moule. He criticized the book's laboured epigrams, but praised the treatment of the women and, again, commended the presentation of rural life; comparison was made with George Eliot's *Silas Marner* and William Barnes's poems in rustic dialect.[15]

Although Hardy, ever sensitive to adverse criticism, remembered the wounding effect of the *Spectator*'s comments, these reviews taken together constituted a reasonably generous appraisal of an anonymous work by a novice. Today, *Desperate Remedies* seems all too redolent of Victorian melodramas, particularly in its coincidences and stagy dialogue. The plotting does verge on the absurd (as when the villain is spied on independently by three furtive observers at the same crucial moment); the generalizations are sometimes banal; and Hardy tends to display learned quotations at inappropriate moments. If the book is read today, it is most likely to be read by students or specialists seeking portents of the mature novelist; and certainly, such portents can be found not only in characterization (Aeneas Manston, the villain, having in common with Alec d'Urberville both a predatory sensuality and a phase of religiosity) but also in description: occasionally a scene is captured with a vividly detailed attention to the play of light, colour and shadow. As the reviewers saw, some of the deftest and most convincing passages render the dialogues of the variously sceptical, shrewd, naïve and genial rural onlookers of the main action.

In June 1871 Hardy was dismayed to find that the three volumes of *Desperate Remedies* were available at the sale price of two shillings and sixpence in the Smith & Son catalogue of surplus books at Exeter station. Nevertheless, Tinsley Brothers sent him a cheque for almost £60, so his net loss was only 'his labour and £15 in money'.[16] One day William Tinsley accosted him in the Strand and, in his bluff cockney manner, asked for another novel: Hardy soon supplied the MS of *Under the Greenwood Tree*, previously deemed by Macmillan to be too slight and short for immediate acceptance. Tinsley paid £30 for general copyright and £10, transmitted from Tauchnitz, for the European copyright. This novel derived partly from *The Poor Man and the Lady* and partly from a tale of rural life that had been meditated three years previously; and Hardy had been encouraged to publish it by the reviewers' emphasis on his talents as a chronicler of countryfolk.

In *Under the Greenwood Tree* he cast aside the melodramatic plotting and contrivance that had characterized *Desperate Remedies* and went to the opposite extreme, offering a gently-paced account of the Stinford Quire and its characters; the plot being minimal, concerning the successful suit of Dick Dewy for the hand of the vivacious village schoolteacher, Fancy Day. Although Hardy did not use the name 'Wessex' in a fictional work until a few years later (in *Far from the Madding Crowd*), this was substantially the first of the 'Wessex' novels, in which Hardy drew heavily on his memories of Bockhampton and on the lives and recollections of village folk there. William Barnes had preceded Hardy in utilizing the name of the old Saxon kingdom to refer to the rural territory of south and south-west England in the nineteenth century;[17] George Eliot, too, would write of 'Wessex' (in *Daniel Deronda*, for instance), and she had anticipated Hardy in her full use of rustic figures, even to the extent of seeking vindication in Dutch realist painting. The discussion of 'these faithful pictures of a monotonous homely existence' in *Adam Bede*, Chapter 17, perhaps suggested the subtitle of *Under the Greenwood Tree*: 'A Rural Painting of the Dutch School'. Nevertheless, Hardy brought a greater mastery of rural idiom, a more intimate knowledge of local custom and folklore, and a keener sensitivity to the relationship between the seasons, the immediate action and the long traditions (now being eroded by cultural innovations) of the countryside. The combination of salty vernacular dialogue, somewhat condescending humour in the depiction of the rustics, realistic detail, a comic-romantic plot ending happily, and, above all, a subtly nostalgic treatment of a gently idealized pastoral community in the heart of the English countryside: all these promised to charm the reviewers, and the promise was kept. The *Athenaeum*, the *Pall Mall Gazette*, the *Spectator* and, predictably, Horace Moule in the *Saturday Review* offered predominantly warm commendation, and the two-volume book sold sufficiently well for Tinsley to decline a bid of £300 for the copyright which had cost him £30. Furthermore, Tinsley was so impressed that he offered Hardy £200 to contribute a serial to *Tinsleys' Magazine*, which impelled the author to rapid work on *A Pair of Blue Eyes*.[18]

This novel drew heavily on Hardy's courtship of Emma, depicting the wild Cornish landscape, a vivacious fair-haired heroine who loves horse-riding, and a suitor of relatively humble parentage who visits the region in order to survey a church which needs rebuilding. The social tensions and frictions caused by class difference (the hero having rural parents, the heroine having a clergyman father with social aspirations) were undoubtedly drawn largely from Hardy's own experiences during his months in Cornwall. Sometimes Emma's very words and ideas, as well as her appearance, were conferred on the enchanting yet unfortunate Elfride of the novel. The cruelly ironic Hardeian plot-pattern was here first deployed. Elfride loves initially the relatively humble suitor, Stephen Smith, and next the older, well-educated middle-class writer, Henry Knight; yet Knight jilts her on learning of her previous love for Stephen. Eventually, both men travel together by train from London to Cornwall, each hoping to win her hand; but the very same train, unknown to them, bears Elfride's coffin, for she has died in childbirth after marrying a landowning widower, Lord Luxellian. Already Hardy is experimenting with a plot-structure so harshly ironic in its coincidences as to give the impression of a cruel destinal force in action. The vivacious heroine, innocently flirtatious, who becomes tragically entangled with two contrasting suitors, anticipates Tess and Sue of the later novels. Notably, Elfride's confession to Henry of her past love for Stephen leads to her harsh rejection by Henry, anticipating Tess's treatment by Angel Clare; while Elfride's decline from eager vitality to depressive disillusionment offers some anticipation of Sue Bridehead's decline.

This novel has various faults of the kind that Hardy long had difficulty in curbing. One is the tendency to 'literariness' in the conversations of the educated people: in particular, Henry Knight tends to speak like an essayist or lecturer, while Elfride is rather implausibly epigrammatical. Coincidental meetings become so frequent as to seem almost routine in this fictional world; the plot resembles an artfully wrought net in which the author seeks to entangle his protagonists. On the other hand, there is a continuation of some of the earlier strengths: the sharply accurate denotation of rural customs and conversation, providing a commentary of pithy and often sceptical common sense; and the acute eye for optical effects, notably the play of light on sea, cloud, and landscape. A new development, too, is the startling juxtaposition of the living present and the vast dead past. Sometimes, admittedly, the juxtaposition is relatively theatrical, as when (in Chapter XXVII) Elfride, arm in arm with Henry, chances to meet her former suitor when they venture into the funeral vault of the Luxellians – where Elfride herself will eventually be buried. On other occasions, the juxtaposition holds the half-didactic, half-visionary distinctiveness of the mature Hardy, as here, when Henry, clinging for life to a cliff-edge, finds himself face to face with a fossilized creature of aeons ago:

By one of those familiar conjunctions of things wherewith the inanimate world baits the mind of man when he pauses in moments of suspense, opposite Knight's eyes was an imbedded fossil, standing forth in low relief from the rock. It was a creature with eyes. The eyes, dead and turned to stone, were even now regarding him. It was one of the early crustaceans called Trilobites. Separated by millions of years in their lives, Knight and this underling seemed to have met in their place of death . . . . .

Time closed up like a fan before him.[19]

With *A Pair of Blue Eyes*, Hardy had advanced considerably in the establishment of his literary identity. After the lurid experiment of

Desperate Remedies and the splendid pastoral experiment of *Under the Greenwood Tree*, the new novel laid the basis for subsequent development. Again and again he would return to the plights of a wandering hero, divided between rural upbringing and middle-class aspiration, and of a heroine whose attractive vivacity leads her into vitiating entanglements; he would use the keenly visualized natural setting which provides a background both supportive and belittling for the central figures; and he would deploy a symmetrical structuring of events which might imply a cosmic mockery of human hopes. This was the first of Hardy's novels to bear his name; and his confidence was vindicated by the reviews, which in the main were warmly enthusiastic. (Again, George Eliot was invoked for comparison: the *Graphic* said, 'Mr. Hardy seems to us to excel everyone but George Eliot'.)[20]

Meanwhile, having read *Under the Greenwood Tree*, Leslie Stephen asked Hardy for a novel to be serialized in *The Cornhill Magazine*. Stephen was an influential essayist and critic; *Cornhill*, which he edited, had a large circulation and high prestige. Its publishers, Smith, Elder & Co., would bring out the novel in volume form near the end of its serialization; and payment would be good: £400, at a time when the average earnings of an adult male in England approximated £56 per year.[21] (£400 in 1873 would be equivalent to approximately £40,000 in 1990.) Hardy had embarked on a literary career at a most propitious time, for the late nineteenth century was a golden era for fiction-writers in Britain. A succession of Education Acts had greatly increased the size of the literate public; numerous publishing houses were being established or expanded to cater for the consequent demands for reading matter; technological advances in printing and in paper production had reduced the costs of books and magazines; literary periodicals burgeoned, providing space for tales and serialized novels; advertising and publicity for authors proliferated; and the space devoted to reviews of novels was (by present standards) enormous. A novelist might then be paid four or five times for the same work: once for its serialization, once for its book form, once again for its publication in Europe, and yet again for its publication in the United States (perhaps in serial as well as in book form); next, after an interval, cheaper reprints might appear. There were additional possibilities: a novel might be adapted for the stage; and later still, after 1910, the author might receive fees from a film company for screen adaptation.

Of course, publication in a magazine often entailed the bowdlerization of a text. Hardy was content to acquiesce in Leslie Stephen's wishes to see *Far from the Madding Crowd* toned down: Fanny Robin's illegitimate baby was not mentioned in the *Cornhill* version. Hardy wrote to him:

I am willing, and indeed anxious, to give up any points which may be desirable in a story when read as a whole, for the sake of others which shall please those who read it in numbers. Perhaps I may have higher aims some day, and be a great stickler for the proper artistic balance of the completed work, but for the present circumstances lead me to wish merely to be considered a good hand at a serial.[22]

Far from the Madding Crowd made Hardy famous: the book, published in 1874, attracted numerous favourable reviews, and sales were rapid. The author was now so prestigious that for his next novel (*The Hand of Ethelberta*), not yet written, he was offered £700 for the English serial and book rights, and £550 for the American serialization in *The New York Times*.[23] These were vast sums by the standards of those days, when a schoolmaster might (like Phillotson) earn £50 per year, and a maidservant only £20. Hardy and his wife could now afford to travel widely in England, with excursions to France, and to take accommodation in London, advancing socially so as to make contact with leading writers and artists of the day. In course of time they were to meet Tennyson, Browning and Matthew Arnold, in addition to numerous members of the gentry and nobility. Yet Hardy could still feel both socially and artistically insecure. Whereas *The Hand of Ethelberta* (1876), a relatively weak novel dealing mainly with middle-class urban life, was well received by the critics, his next novel, the far more powerful *Return of the Native* (1878), incurred reproaches from several reviewers for its 'gloomy fatalism'. The pessimism which derived partly from his general reflections on life, partly from incidents like the suicide of his friend Horace Moule in 1873, and which was gradually accentuated by his alienation from his wife, was already colouring his work in dark hues that troubled and sometimes repelled its critics. As he confided to his Journal:

Law [i.e. the evolutionary process] has produced in man a child who cannot but constantly reproach its parent for doing much and yet not all, and constantly say to such parent that it would have been better never to have begun doing than to have *over*done so indecisively . . . . . on the emotional side . . . . .

If Law itself had consciousness, how the aspect of its creatures would terrify it, fill it with remorse![24]

In 1880, when *The Trumpet-Major* (a novel of Napoleonic times) appeared, Hardy was taken ill with a mysterious malaise and was bedridden for six months; nevertheless he managed to complete *A Laodicean*, which received aptly Laodicean but generally respectful reviews. He bought land near Dorchester and had a house (Max Gate) built there for himself to his own design, his father being the chief builder. Max Gate, completed in 1885, remained his home to the end of his life, though he frequently resided in London for part of the year. During the subsequent three years he published one of his greatest novels, *The Mayor of Casterbridge*, the more modest though quite successful work *The Woodlanders*, and his first collection of short stories, *Wessex Tales*.

A second collection of tales, *A Group of Noble Dames*, appeared in 1891 but was overshadowed in that year by the storm of controversy over *Tess of the d'Urbervilles*. Following rejections by various magazines, *Tess* was published by the *Graphic* only after extensive bowdlerization: Tess's rape by Alex was replaced by a sham marriage; her illegitimate child was not mentioned; and, ludicrously (in response to a plea from the *Graphic*'s editor), Angel was obliged to carry the dairymaids across the flood not in his arms but in a wheelbarrow. The book version restored the sexual frankness of the original. Reviews were numerous and widely divergent. Some (like the *Quarterly*) condemned the book as immoral both in its defence of the wronged Tess as 'a pure woman' and in its pessimism. Many other reviewers, however, like those in the *Athenaeum*, *The Times*, the *Pall Mall Gazette* and the *Daily Chronicle*, saw it as immensely powerful and tragic. Controversy, particularly over the sexual content, was then (as it is now) a likely guarantor of a novel's sales; and sales of *Tess* far surpassed those of the earlier works. R. G. Cox reports:

Of the three-volume edition of *Tess* two further impressions of 500 each had succeeded the first 1,000 within four months. The one-volume reprint at 6s [six shillings] ran to five impressions totalling 17,000 between September 1892 and the end of the year.[25]

The novel was soon translated into French, German, Dutch, Italian, Polish and Russian, and between 1900 and 1930 was reprinted 'some forty times in England alone'. Macmillan published 226,750 copies between 1895 and 1929; furthermore, 100,000 copies of the paperback edition by Harper were issued, giving Hardy one penny royalty for every sixpenny copy sold.[26] The scandalous *Tess* ensured Hardy's prosperity.

There was a similar pattern to the reception of *Jude the Obscure*, which was the most deeply personal novel of 'Thomas the Unworthy', as he called himself.[27] Into it he had put his recollections of Tryphena Sparks, his disillusionment with marriage, the sense of regret that he had not entered a university, his conviction that the evolutionary process had generated humans too sensitive for the world in which they must exist, and his belief that outdated institutions and ideas fettered and oppressed individual liberty. Wearing the mask, however transparent, of the fictional narrator and orchestrator, Hardy could speak more fiercely and bitterly than in any avowedly autobiographical work; and in no previous novel had he dared to challenge so directly and widely the shibboleths of Victorianism. Predictably, the hostility to *Jude the Obscure* was even more vehement and widespread than to *Tess*. In compliance with requests from the editor of *Harper's Magazine*, Hardy had bowdlerized the serial to the extent of making parts of the plot virtually incomprehensible; but when the book appeared in 1895, the Bishop of Wakefield claimed to have burnt his copy ('probably in his despair at not being able to burn me', commented Hardy) and arranged for the major circulating library (Smith's) to ban the novel from its shelves.[28] The *Pall Mall Gazette* attacked 'Jude the Obscene'; the *Fortnightly Review* and *National Review* inveighed against the book's sexual frankness; and *Blackwood's* assigned Hardy to 'The Anti-Marriage League'.[29] Radical or 'progressive' papers, predictably, were generally sympathetic or laudatory; but the author was inclined rather to smart under the lash of the harsher reviews than to bask in the glow of the sanguine.

Hardy claimed that the uncomprehending, hostile press reception of *Tess* and particularly of *Jude* 'compelled him . . . . . if he wished to retain any shadow of self-respect' to abandon novel-writing in favour of his first literary love, poetry.[30] There was an ideological reason, too: Hardy observed ruefully that ideas which would provoke a storm if expressed in prose seemed to be tolerated if expressed in verse. 'If Galileo had said in verse that the world moved, the Inquisition might have let him alone.'[31] It is certainly the case that he had long been meditating an epic verse-drama on the Napoleonic wars: this eventually appeared as *The Dynasts*. It was also obvious, however, that the controversies over *Tess* and *Jude* had greatly increased both his fame and the sales of his novels. In England alone, 20,000 copies of *Jude* were marketed within three months, and between 1896 and 1929 Macmillan sold over 109,000 copies; sales in the United States were also large. (Hardy was now able to stipulate a royalty as high as 20 per cent.)[32] Accordingly, his prosperity as a writer was now assured; he could afford to relinquish the struggle to sell vendible copy to magazine-editors and publishers.

2.3 Subsequent Years

A relatively slight novel which had been written in the 1880s, *The Well-Beloved*, was published in 1897, and this was the last of his novels to emerge. A final collection of tales, *A Changed Man*, appeared in 1913. Otherwise, for the remainder of his life, Hardy concentrated on poetry. The immense experimental verse-drama, *The Dynasts*, emerged in stages: Part I, 1904; Part II, 1906; Part III, 1908. The initial critical reaction was generally unfavourable; though, as the subsequent parts appeared, more voices were raised in its defence, *The Times Literary Supplement* even claiming that it rivalled Shakespeare's historical plays.[33] From time to time attempts were made to perform parts of the work in the theatre; but over the years the consensus has grown that *The Dynasts*, however bold, ambitious and proleptic (anticipating the attempted revival of verse-drama by Eliot, Auden, Fry and others in the 1930s), is an experiment which failed. Similarly, his verse-play *The Famous Tragedy of the Queen of Cornwall* (1923) remains seldom read and very seldom performed.

Hardy's volumes of short poems, however, soon established themselves as a rich and distinctive opus which included many fine and memorable items: 'The Darkling Thrush', 'Beeny Cliff', 'Drummer Hodge', 'The Oxen' and 'In Time of "The Breaking of Nations"' became celebrated anthology-pieces, and Hardy was gratified by the acclaim given him by younger poets (particularly the 'Georgians') who saw him as a mentor and master. After his death, his poems were acclaimed by Ezra Pound, sympathetically appraised by W. H. Auden, and exerted a marked influence on Philip Larkin. Another poet, Donald Davie, even affirmed (over-enthusiastically) that Hardy was the greatest single influence on British poetry in the period 1923–73.[34]

Though, as an infant, Hardy had seemed frail and puny, he proved later to be remarkably resilient, enjoying lengthy bicycle-rides in his sixties and seventies; and, after the storm and stress of the controversies over his novels, he survived to bask in the praise and honour granted to a distinguished English 'Man of Letters'. In 1909 he was awarded the Order of Merit and the freedom of Dorchester; later, honorary doctorates were conferred on him by both Cambridge and Oxford, so the 'Christminster' which had rejected Jude the Obscure now gave its accolade to Hardy the Illustrious. Meanwhile, his unhappy first marriage ended with the sudden death of Emma in 1912. Fifteen months later, he married his secretary and assistant, Florence Emily Dugdale, who cooperated with him in producing that biography which was largely a lightly disguised autobiography in which the author looks back with some pardonable self-satisfaction on his struggles and achievements.

When he died in 1928, his ashes were interred in the Poets' Corner of Westminster Abbey, while his heart was buried at Stinsford, in the grave of his first wife and next to that of his parents. This double interment had an obvious symbolic aptness. Hardy, the acclaimed national writer, celebrator of the English countryside and its traditions, had become so important a part of the cultural heritage that Westminster Abbey required his presence; yet his emotional loyalty to the humble locality of his early upbringing, coupled with his nostalgia for the early years of happiness with his first wife, made Stinsford seem appropriate too. Indeed, it could be said that that double interment finally resolved the tension which runs through all his literary work: that tension between urban and rural, between the cultural claims of advanced civilization and the claims of the humble but essential community of the toilers in the fields and in the streets.

After the 1914–18 war, though sales of the novels increased, there was a relative decline in Hardy's reputation as the radical works of Eliot, Pound, Joyce and Lawrence became the centre of literary debate; and, following his death, sales declined markedly, while critical hostility was sharp in some quarters: Eliot himself spoke rather sneeringly of Hardy in *After Strange Gods*. Nevertheless, Middleton Murry and F. R. Leavis helped to give some of Hardy's poems a 'canonical' status. Though Leavis excluded Hardy from the so-called 'Great Tradition' of major novelists, history has mocked such exclusiveness. In the later decades of the twentieth century, Hardy was commonly ranked with Conrad as a crucial figure in the cultural transition from Victorianism to Modernism; his novels had become the centre of a vast and growing industry of critical and scholarly analysis; and, thanks largely to the cinema and television, which brought Bathsheba, Tess and Jude before audiences of many millions, the novels, regaining popularity, displayed remarkable staying power, circulating in paperback to a wide popular readership as well as serving the requirements of schools and colleges. Even within his lifetime, the cinema industry had helped to guarantee Hardy's influence as well as his prosperity: early films of *Tess* appeared in 1913 and 1924, *Far from the Madding Crowd* in 1911 and 1915, and *The Mayor of Casterbridge* in 1921. Films made since his death include *Under the Greenwood Tree*, 1929, and, after a significant long hiatus, John Schlesinger's *Far from the Madding Crowd*, 1967, and Roman Polanski's *Tess*, 1979. Television producers in Britain were slow to appreciate Hardy's potential but eventually made amends; and, given that such British programmes were often sold to foreign networks, they handsomely augmented the author's fame. The tale 'The Distracted Preacher' was televised in 1969; *The Woodlanders* followed in 1970 (repeated 1971); *Jude the Obscure*, dramatized by Harry Green, with Robert Powell as a convincing Jude, appeared in 1971; a six-part series, 'Wessex Tales', was shown in 1973 and repeated in 1975; and a serial version of *The Mayor of Casterbridge* (dramatized by Dennis Potter) was shown in 1978 and repeated in 1979. On television and radio there have been numerous readings of the poems. Most of the novels have received repeated readings or dramatizations, though *Under the Greenwood Tree*, *The Trumpet-Major*, *Far from the Madding Crowd*, *The Woodlanders*, *The Mayor of Casterbridge* and *Tess* have all gained markedly more attention than *Jude*.[35] Euan Smith's adaptation of *Jude* for the theatre was successfully staged at the Young Vic in 1990.

The influence on other writers has been diverse. In Hardy's lifetime, Marcel Proust wrote sympathetically about him in *A la recherche du temps perdu*, and Hardy noted the affinities in their treatment of desire and memory;[36] D. H. Lawrence's novels (as the *Study of Thomas Hardy* amply suggested) often resembled an argumentative extension of Hardy's preoccupations; and in 1977 John Fowles's essay, 'Hardy and the Hag', provided a reminder of the profound influence of Hardy's poetry and prose on the author of that brilliant rediscovery of Wessex, *The French Lieutenant's Woman* (1969).[37] (In the penultimate chapter of *The Return of the Native*, Hardy had offered his readers two alternative endings. When Fowles adopted this device ninety-one years later, it was regarded as a 'Post-modernist' innovation.) By the end of the twentieth century, Thomas Hardy had become not only a celebrated major author but also a cultural phenomenon, a magnet to the tourist trade, a brand-name for depictions of rural England in the nineteenth century, a figure venerated by British patriots, the *raison d'être* of a literary society with its *Thomas Hardy Journal*, an ideal topic for a 'Media Studies' course, and even an image gracing the pump-handles of a draught beer sold in London pubs.

Literary criticism is still striving to come to terms with the strange and rich power of his writing: the tensions, oddities, eloquences; the mixture of nostalgia and harsh irony, of radical challenge and pessimistic stoicism; his modes of conventionality and his astonishing defiances of convention. Feminist critics are steadily discovering the extent to which the debates on sexual politics of the late twentieth century were thoroughly anticipated by Hardy in the late nineteenth. His imaginative and linguistic resourcefulness makes it seem likely that he will long outflank any critic who hopes to achieve a 'definitive' estimate. He retains the capacity to surprise, to enlighten and to move: 'move' in that he can still evoke a powerful emotional response; 'move' in that, at his best, as in *Jude the Obscure*, he can strike to the side of the expected, catching life from an unfamiliar angle, and catching us too in the mesh of his mobile responsiveness.

2.4 Autobiographical Features of *Jude the Obscure*

Part 2 began by citing Hardy's avowal that there was 'not a scrap of personal detail' in *Jude the Obscure*. The subsequent account of his life has, on the contrary, emphasized ways in which he repeatedly drew on personal experience when writing the novel. Hardy's two frustrated ambitions, to enter both the University and the Church, are also Jude's (and Phillotson's). The unhappiness of Hardy's first marriage has evidently influenced the treatment of Jude's marital wretchedness and the jaundiced view of marriage in general; and the conflict between Hardy's scepticism and his wife's increasing pietism is given dramatic accentuation in the text.[38] Hardy's sense of social deracination and insecurity has contributed to Jude's situation as one who is sufficiently educated to be culturally superior to the folk of his rural origins, yet who lacks the means to be readily accepted in middle-class circles. Even the childhood fears of adult life as ominous and disruptive ('If he could only prevent himself growing up!') are common to Jude and his author.[39]

Carl J. Weber's study, *Hardy of Wessex*, has listed numerous small but telling linkages between the author and the protagonist of *Jude*.[40] Both are bookworms who study Clarke's Homer and Griesbach's Greek New Testament; both make telling quotations from Buckley's translation of Aeschylus; Jude shares Hardy's view that Salisbury Cathedral is 'the most graceful architectural pile in England'; both are intensely moved by organ music; and Jude quotes Hardy's favourite poem by Browning, 'The Statue and the Bust'. Both men find the Book of Job all too appropriate a commentary on their disappointments in life. The surname 'Fawley' derives from Great Fawley, the village in Berkshire where the author's grandmother had endured hardship.

Weber speculates that the warnings given to Jude about the dangers of marrying a cousin may have resembled those given to Hardy in 1868 when he was 'walking out' with his cousin Tryphena Sparks. After Tryphena died in 1890, Hardy went to call on her daughter; thus he anticipated Jude's reflection: 'If at the . . . . . death of my lost love, I could go and see her child . . . . . there would be comfort in it!' [41] Hardy acknowledged that Tryphena's death had partly prompted the 'scheme' of the novel.[42] Hardy's sisters, Mary and Kate, had studied at the Teachers' Training School at Salisbury; he had visited them there; and the visit doubtless contributed to his hostile description of that 'species of nunnery known as the Training School at Melchester' which Sue attends.

More important than such local details, however, is the fact that the ideological tensions and conflicts which energize the novel derive so evidently from Hardy's personal experience of class conflict and injustice, of religious aspiration and disillusionment, of the moral hypocrisies and double standards in late Victorian England, and of 'a deadly war waged between flesh and spirit'[43] within the evolutionary hybrid, man: the creature so often divided between noble idealism and demeaning desire. Such tensions will be discussed in Part 3 of this book.

If Hardy exaggerated the distance between himself and the contents of the novel, that may have been because he recognized that the author is both more and less than the self implied by the work. 'More', because the author can generate alternative fictions and thus alternative implied selves; 'more', too, because the 'omniscient narrator' of a text has a character inflected by the nature of the material to be narrated; and 'less', because the demands and disciplines of creative writing engender qualities of articulacy, intelligence and insight that might never otherwise emerge from the self that has chosen to take up the pen. *Jude the Obscure* doubtless expresses oblique self-pity, personal bitterness and even vengefulness; yet literary disciplines have served to complicate, refine, contest and generalize such feelings, so that the text can speak cogently on behalf of many people, then and now, in many tones, ranging from the satiric to the elegiac.

Part 3 Sources and Contexts of *Jude the Obscure*

Part 2 noted some ways in which Hardy's 'personal experience', conventionally defined, contributed to *Jude the Obscure*. A broader definition of 'personal experience' would, however, emphasize the ways in which this novel derives its richness and radicalism from Hardy's responsiveness to the numerous ideas, preoccupations and controversies of his era. Henry James once referred patronizingly to the author as 'The good little Thomas Hardy';[1] but, in his responsiveness to social, sexual, political and cultural matters, Hardy had an imaginative magnitude which makes Henry James seem, at times, parochially limited.

Understandably, given his social and cultural situation, Hardy was often a Janiform writer.[2] His tutelary deity frequently seems to be the god Janus, the two-faced god who looks in opposite directions at the same time (and who provides the name of janitors and January); for Hardy was inwardly divided – pulled and pushed in conflicting ways. We can relate this duplicity partly to his social position: a man from the class of rural artisans who moved amongst the intelligentsia and gentry of the city; a scholar and autodidact who could look critically both on the philistinism of the labouring class and on the prosperous life of the university-educated middle and upper classes of London; a man who yet anxiously sought acceptance in fashionable social circles, while harbouring fierce resentments at the injustices of the social system which gave easy advantages and privileges to a favoured few. He was receptive to some of the most radical ideas of his time, but preserved a defensive scepticism and resilient pessimism.

A concise list of the resultant tensions in *Jude the Obscure* might be this:

1. Society is gradually becoming more liberal and tolerant; yet society increasingly oppresses the sensitive.
2. In the future, life may be better for the aspiring Judes and Sues; yet, in that future, such people may be extinct.
3. Sexuality may bring joyous fulfilment; yet sexuality tortures and demeans the idealistic.
4. Culture is desirable and liberating; yet culture is a false god nurtured by privilege.
5. Reflectiveness brings wisdom; yet ignorance is bliss.
6. Evolution is progressive; yet evolution engenders woeful awareness.

22

7. God is non-existent; yet a callous or stupid Will ordains events.

Jude the Obscure, accordingly, is a Janiform text: in important areas it is not merely ambiguous or complex but moves towards paradox and even self-contradiction. Vigorously structured in its narrative patterns and powerfully sombre in its general tenor, the novel nevertheless displays an ideological volatility. The author is entangled in some of the confusions which he boldly seeks to describe, define and explain. Thus *Jude*, for all its architectural symmetry of plotting, reveals marked variability in its moral and philosophical outlook. The following sections discuss that variability.

3.1 Evolutionary Theories

In his imagination, Hardy was a time-traveller and space-traveller. Hence the astonishing shifts in perspective which repeatedly enrich his descriptions. He describes an object as it appears now, and then invokes a vast historical perspective in which that object is part of an ages-long continuum. He describes closely a figure in a given location, and next gives a bird's-eye view as though that figure were seen from remote heights. The object or figure first looms large and then is diminished or transformed in significance. The shifts in perspective are linked to shifts in valuation; hence that sense of narratorial mobility and fluctuating sympathy, for now we are sympathetically close and now taking a detached and Olympian view.

When Hardy is writing most interestingly, there often occur such moments when a character who has previously loomed large in the foreground is suddenly diminished by the invocation of a vast perspective of space or time or both. As an extreme instance, we may think of Knight, in *A Pair of Blue Eyes*, clinging to the lofty cliff and facing a fossilized trilobite, and realizing his insignificance as just another creature in the aeons-long evolutionary process. In *Jude the Obscure*, Jude looks glumly into a well; the narrator remarks that it was 'as ancient as the village itself', so that as Jude looks down into its depths the narrator is looking back into history. Later, the young lad makes his way across a dreary expanse of harrowed field which to him is empty and silent; but the narrator populates it with the sounds and actions of centuries of rural life:

[I]n every clod and stone there really lingered associations enough and to spare – echoes of songs from ancient harvest-days, of spoken words, and of sturdy deeds. Every inch of ground had been the site, first or last, of energy, gaiety,

23

horse-play, bickerings, weariness. Groups of gleaners had squatted in the sun on every square yard. Love-matches that had populated the adjoining hamlet had been made up there between reaping and carrying.[3]

For Hardy, a natural continuum linked the historical, the archaeological and the evolutionary perspectives. Notions of evolution repeatedly influence his scenic imagination, his views of character and heredity, his pessimism and his metaphysic. In different ways, numerous other writers of the late nineteenth century were time-travellers, too: we may think of William Morris's *News from Nowhere*, of H. G. Wells's *The Time Machine*, or Joseph Conrad's *Heart of Darkness*. Repeatedly such authors saw present individuals as part of an extensive drama which began aeons in the past and continues into a remote, problematic future.

Evolutionary theories of various kinds have abounded throughout history; but in the nineteenth century they gained powerful emphasis from empirical science. Darwin's *Origin of Species* (1859) was part of a trend: Darwin acknowledged his indebtedness both to Thomas Malthus's theory of population (1798–1826) and to Sir Charles Lyell's *Principles of Geology* (1830–33). Geological investigation undermined the Christian beliefs that the world had been created relatively recently (in 4004 BC, according to Bishop Ussher), that man was a special creation and that the creative process was overseen by a benevolent God. The earth proved to be many millions of years old, and fossil evidence (collected with assiduity by numerous researchers in the Victorian age) revealed that whole species had appeared and become extinct in course of the vast struggle with the changing environment. Astronomy, too, by revealing further and further reaches of space, galaxy beyond galaxy, augmented that cosmically reductive perspective on humanity. Tennyson's *In Memoriam*, which grapples at length with the enormity of the moral and theological problems presented by evolutionary discoveries, antedates *The Origin of Species* but is strongly influenced by Lyell's work. With a sombre intensity which was to re-echo in Hardy's pages, Tennyson reflected thus:

> Are God and Nature then at strife,
>   That Nature lends such evil dreams?
>   So careful of the type she seems,
> So careless of the single life . . . . .
>
> 'So careful of the type?' but no.
>   From scarped cliff and quarried stone
>   She cries, 'A thousand types are gone;
> I care for nothing, all shall go.

'Thou makest thine appeal to me.
  I bring to life, I bring to death;
  The spirit does but mean the breath;
I know no more.' And he, shall he,

Man, her last work, who seem'd so fair,
  Such splendid purpose in his eyes,
  Who roll'd the psalm to wintry skies,
Who built him fanes of fruitless prayer,

Who trusted God was love indeed
  And love Creation's final law –
  Tho' Nature, red in tooth and claw
With ravine, shriek'd against his creed –

Who lov'd, who suffer'd countless ills,
  Who battled for the True, the Just,
  Be blown about the desert dust,
Or seal'd within the iron hills?[4]

Already, therefore, the way was prepared for the daunting authority of Darwin's *Origin of Species*, which accounted for evolutionary change by postulating 'natural selection' as the ruthless mechanism. Furthermore, his *Descent of Man* (1871) offered proofs of man's simian ancestry: man was no longer lord of the earthly creation, mediating between animals and angels, but merely a reflective part of the animal world. As Joseph Conrad would remark:

What makes mankind tragic is not that they are the victims of nature, it is that they are conscious of it. To be part of the animal kingdom under the conditions of this earth is very well – but as soon as you know of your slavery the pain, the anger, the strife – the tragedy begins.[5]

Of course, evolutionary notions could permit optimistic as well as pessimistic glosses. Darwin himself, in the peroration of *The Origin of Species*, had proffered an optimistic gloss by proclaiming a progressive tendency:

[A]s natural selection works solely by and for the good of each being, all corporeal and mental endowments will tend to progress towards perfection.

It is interesting to contemplate an entangled bank, clothed with many plants of many kinds, with birds singing on the bushes, with various insects flitting about, and with worms crawling through the damp earth, and to reflect that these elaborately constructed forms, so different from each other, and dependent on each other in so complex a manner, have all been produced by laws acting around us. These laws . . . . . being Growth with Reproduction; Inheritance . . . . .; Variability . . . . .; a Ratio of Increase so high as to lead to a Struggle for Life, and as a consequence to Natural Selection, entailing Divergence of Character and the Extinction of less-improved forms. Thus, from the war of nature, from famine and death, the most exalted object which we are capable of conceiving, namely, the production of the higher animals, directly follows. There is grandeur in this view of life, with its several powers, having been originally breathed into a few forms or into one; and that, whilst this planet has gone cycling on according to the fixed law of gravity, from so simple a beginning endless forms most beautiful and wonderful have been, and are being, evolved.[6]

Hardy said that he had been 'among the earliest acclaimers of *The Origin of Species*',[7] and his writings repeatedly bear witness to this statement; but Darwin's meliorism is frequently challenged by them. Markedly, Hardy stresses the bitterness of the 'Struggle for Life' and the destructiveness of 'the war of nature'. 'O why should Nature's law be mutual butchery!' cries Sue.[8] Darwin had looked appreciatively on the 'worms crawling through the damp earth'; the young Jude, beholding 'scores of coupled earthworms lying half their length on the surface of the damp ground', found that 'It was impossible to advance in regular steps without crushing some of them at each tread'; so, with exquisite sensitivity, 'He carefully picked his way on tiptoe among the earthworms, without killing a single one.' Indeed, this sensitivity is a 'weakness of character, as it may be called':

[H]e was a boy who could not himself bear to hurt anything. He had never brought home a nest of young birds without lying awake in misery half the night after, and often reinstating them and the nest in their original place the next morning. He could scarcely bear to see trees cut down or lopped, from a fancy that it hurt them . . . . .[9]

Here is a sensitivity which is, in part, a relic of primitive animism – the belief that each part of nature has a spirit or soul; but Hardy, the supporter of the RSPCA (Royal Society for the Prevention of Cruelty to Animals), knew that Darwinism had given new, if demeaning, warrant to the sense that man was on a par with other living creatures, and thus provided strong justification to humans who sought to be more humane to their fellow-denizens of the earth. So the older Jude, wincing when his dying pig looks at him with apparent reproach, tries to cut short its agony; later he goes out at night, on hearing a squealing rabbit in a trap, to put it out of its misery; and Sue (who thinks of herself as a 'bird . . . . . caught')[10] guiltily releases a poulterer's pigeons before they can be sold as food.

Meliorist versions of evolutionary theory were offered by numerous writers: by Tennyson, for example, who, near the end of *In Memoriam*, imagined that people might eventually transcend their bestial heritage and emerge as a higher type of being, wise and serene. In France, Count de Saint-Simon, founder of French socialism, had envisaged a combination of primitive Christianity with scientific and industrial progress; and his ideas influenced Auguste Comte, whose 'Positivism' advocated a 'Religion of Humanity' in which the noblest representatives of mankind serve as saints to inspire the others to greater endeavours. Comte believed that in the race and in the individual there are three stages of cultural evolution: in the first or theological stage there is a belief in gods, spirits and myths; in the second or metaphysical stage the futilities of abstract philosophizing are dominant; and in the third, highest and 'positive' stage, man concentrates on material reality and scientific classifications. The membership of Jude's Artizans' Society includes Positivists. Clym Yeobright, in *The Return of the Native*, has possibly been influenced by Saint-Simon and Comte, but his career and setbacks form a sceptical comment on the doctrines. Frederic Harrison thought that *Tess of the d'Urbervilles* resembled 'a Positivist allegory or sermon'.[11]

In *Jude the Obscure*, which is certainly Hardy's bleakest novel, there is an element of tension or contradiction created by the tug of meliorist notions against a dominant pessimism. Thomas Hardy, who often sought to combat critical clichés about his outlook, sometimes denied that he was a pessimist: he simply served the truth, he claimed; and if the truth he recorded seemed frequently to be tragic, it did not follow that he was unaware of 'a contrasting side of things'.[12] One meliorist suggestion in *Jude* is that both Jude himself and Sue are, in terms of human and social evolution, 'ahead of their times': if they could have lived in a future era, their plight would not have been so lonely and beleaguered, because there would then have been more fellow-beings able to share their enlightenment and sensitivity, and social progress would have made the world more congenial to them. 'Our ideas were fifty years too soon', reflects Jude, and notes that 'soon there is going to be a better chance for such helpless students as I was . . . . .'[13] Yet, in stark contrast to that sense that social evolution is making conditions better for the Judes and Sues of the future, the text also voices a Schopenhauerian prophecy that in the future there will be no Judes and Sues, for the sensitive will prefer to perish.

Arthur Schopenhauer (1788–1860), a philosopher respected by Hardy,[14] bleakly declared:

[C]hildren can sometimes seem like innocent delinquents, sentenced not to death but to life, who have not yet discovered what their punishment will consist of . . . . .

If you imagine . . . . . the sum total of distress, pain and suffering of every kind which the sun shines upon in its course, you will have to admit it would have been much better if the sun had been able to call up the phenomenon of life as little on the earth as on the moon . . . . .

You can also look upon our life as an episode unprofitably disturbing the blessed calm of nothingness. In any case, even he who has found life tolerably bearable will, the longer he lives, feel the more clearly that on the whole it is a disappointment, nay a cheat . . . . .

If the act of procreation were neither the outcome of a desire nor accompanied by feelings of pleasure, but a matter to be decided on the basis of purely rational considerations, is it likely the human race would still exist? Would each of us not rather have felt so much pity for the coming generation as to prefer to spare it the burden of existence . . . . .?[15]

This dismal notion seems to be echoed in *Jude*, in the aftermath of the death of Jude's children:

'The doctor says there are such boys springing up amongst us – boys of a sort unknown in the last generation – the outcome of new views of life. They seem to see all its terrors before they are old enough to have staying power to resist them. He says it is the beginning of the coming universal wish not to live. He's an advanced man, the doctor . . . . .'[16]

Thus, on the one hand, there is the idea that Jude and Sue are forerunners of a more sensitive humanity for which the future society might prove more congenial; and, on the other hand, there is the starkly contrasting idea that, as sensitive human beings become more aware of the irremediable wretchedness of the human plight, observers note the onset of a 'universal wish not to live' – an erasure of an evolutionary mistake. The young Jude, we are told, seemed 'born to ache a good deal before the fall of the curtain upon his unnecessary life should signify that all was well with him again'.[17]

A related aspect of Hardy's preoccupation with evolutionary ideas is his deep ambivalence about sexual desires. The preface to the novel stated that it concerned, among other matters, 'the strongest passion known to humanity[, and] a deadly war waged between flesh and spirit'.[18] Jude's spiritual and educational aspirations are disrupted by his seduction by Arabella; he reproaches himself bitterly for letting his sexual desires overcome his higher ideals. It is as though he is an evolutionary hybrid, mentally advanced in humanity yet biologically chained to the bestial world. Yet, when Jude suffers agonies of frustration during his relationship with the virginal Sue, the matter becomes markedly more ambivalent. Partly, the authorial viewpoint is sympathetic to Jude, who is given some telling lines of expostulation; and, partly, it is sympathetic to Sue. There are many possible explanations of her sexual 'inhibitions'; one is that in an evolutionary scale she has advanced further than the menfolk in her world, so that she is less governed by the carnal than they, who repeatedly demean what might potentially be a 'higher', 'purer' kind of love. So here, again, is a radical ambivalence in the text. In some respects, the novel advocates a sexually liberated time, when the desires are not fettered by conventional ties of 'holy wedlock' and lovers may live freely together; or, as Sue puts it: 'I said it was Nature's intention, Nature's law and *raison d'être* that we should be joyful in what instincts she afforded us – instincts which civilization had taken upon itself to thwart.'[19] William Blake and D. H. Lawrence might have approved her claim. Nevertheless, in opposition to this liberal advocacy of spontaneity in sexual commitment, the novel places heavy emphasis not on the joys and fulfilments but on the betrayals, the frictions and coercions caused by the sexual impulses, which form part of that meshwork of 'gins and springes' which make a Laocoön – a serpentine entanglement – for struggling individuals; and Jude's children perish wretchedly, as if to confirm Phillotson's grim assertion that 'Cruelty is the law pervading all nature and society'.[20]

3.2 Religion and Scepticism

In religious matters, Hardy is again Janiform: paradoxical and even self-contradictory. His attitudes include the agnostic, the atheistic, the antitheistic, the nostalgic, and what he termed the 'churchy';[21] and, furthermore, he conceived an evolutionary theology which was both distinctively Hardeian and clearly of its times. Once again, Hardy's non-fictional pronouncements are often strongly defensive, a reaction against those critics who had condemned his apparently heretical outlook:

Positive views on the Whence and the Wherefore of things have never been advanced by this pen as a consistent philosophy . . . . . [T]he sentiments in the following pages have been stated truly to be mere impressions of the moment, and not convictions or arguments.[22]

As usual, there is a valid point here: all ideas offered within works of fiction are ideas 'in quotation marks': as part of a fictional world, they are implicitly hypothetical. Yet, if certain ideas are recurrent and vigorous in an author's fictional output, they tend to form a significant part of the imaginative identity of that output, and may do so to such an extent that it would seem pedantic to evade the convention of referring to them as 'Hardy's ideas'.

Agnosticism, the belief that humans cannot know whether there is or is not a God, has been available in various forms since ancient times; it may be traced back, for example, to the radical scepticism of Pyrrho of Elis (*circa* 365–275 BC). The term 'agnosticism' itself (derived from the Greek *a*, not, and *gnostikos*, good at knowing) was first coined in 1869 by Thomas Huxley, the famous advocate of Darwinism. Hardy referred to himself as 'a harmless agnostic'; but that claim was repeatedly belied by the vigour with which he voiced atheistic and antitheistic sentiments. Indeed, the context of his claim aptly illustrates this point:

To cry out in a passionate poem that (for instance) the Supreme Mover or Movers, the Prime Force or Forces, must be either limited in power, unknowing, or cruel – which is obvious enough, and has been for centuries – will cause them [i.e. 'the vast body of men'] merely a shake of the head; but to put it in argumentative prose will make them sneer, or foam, and set all the literary contortionists jumping upon me, a harmless agnostic, as if I were a clamorous atheist, which in their crass illiteracy they seem to think is the same thing . . . [23]

In the very act of describing himself as an agnostic and not an atheist, he concedes that the ideas which he wishes to 'cry out' include the idea that 'the Supreme Mover' is 'either limited in power, unknowing, or cruel' – a range which includes the antitheistic.

Hostile critics had indeed seized indignantly on the statement in the final paragraph of *Tess of the d'Urbervilles*: ' "Justice" was done, and the President of the Immortals, in Aeschylean phrase, had ended his sport with Tess.' Hardy claimed that the critics had naïvely misinterpreted a poetic figure of speech; he was not really imputing cruelty to a 'man-shaped tribal god'.[24] Nevertheless, the 'Aeschylean phrase' does sum up quite aptly the impressions created by various features of the text; Tess does seem to have been so repeatedly caught and tormented as to be a victim not only of human agency but also of 'the Supreme Mover'. In his non-fictional declarations, Hardy may not have recognized the extent to which his theoretical distinctions tended to be blurred by the intensity of his theological and moral indignations.

This point can be well illustrated by one of Hardy's earliest poems:

Hap

If but some vengeful god would call to me
From up the sky, and laugh: 'Thou suffering thing,

Know that thy sorrow is my ecstasy,
That thy love's loss is my hate's profiting!'

Then would I bear it, clench myself, and die,
Steeled by the sense of ire unmerited;
Half-eased in that a Powerfuller than I
Had willed and meted me the tears I shed.

But not so. How arrives it joy lies slain,
And why unblooms the best hope ever sown?
– Cross Casualty obstructs the sun and rain,
And dicing Time for gladness casts a moan . . .
These purblind Doomsters had as readily strown
Blisses about my pilgrimage as pain.[25]

The poem denies the existence of a hostile, vengeful god, and says that instead there are only 'purblind Doomsters' – 'Cross Casualty' (stupid chance) and 'dicing Time'. It says that these impersonal forces could as readily have given happiness as wretchedness. Nevertheless, the clear drift of the poem is that, in fact, the speaker has known wretchedness rather than happiness. He might even have found consolation (been 'Half-eased') in recognizing a hostile god; that would have made moral sense of the suffering. Instead, there have been merely these impersonal forces at work. Yet, in the very act of describing their actions and providing personifying capitalizations ('Casualty', 'Time', 'Doomsters'), the poet makes them sound not wholly unlike that hostile god: they are powerful and, in his case, callous, for they have slain joy and made hope 'unbloom'. In short, what the poem vigorously suggests (in its contorted, gnarled and forceful phrasing) blurs the logical distinction it purports to be defining.

Whereas an agnostic claims that we cannot know that there is or is not a God, and an atheist asserts that there is no God, the antitheist claims that God exists but is uncaring or malevolent instead of benevolent. The poem 'Hap' dismisses, though with a certain reluctance, the antitheistic notion; but, though we expect it to endorse the agnostic or atheistical notion, it offers a view of unwittingly harsh, unthinkingly cruel forces – which are not unlike, in the consequences they have bestowed, a cruel God, except that since they are unwitting, there is no malice aforethought. Yet the inflictions on the suffering individual remain the same. In a letter to Alfred Noyes, Hardy denied claiming 'that the Power behind the universe is malign': 'the said Cause is neither moral nor immoral, but *un*moral'; 'The Scheme of Things is, indeed, incomprehensible'.[26] Nevertheless, a journal entry for 10 December 1888 had blended the notion of the *unknowing* Cause with that of the *sinning* Cause:

He, she, had blundered; but not as the Prime Cause had blundered. He, she, had sinned; but not as the Prime Cause had sinned. He, she, was ashamed and sorry; but not as the Prime Cause would be ashamed and sorry if it knew.[27]

In the nineteenth and early twentieth centuries, the religious heritage was so powerful in Europe that even those thinkers who sceptically rebelled against religion often experienced difficulty in emancipating themselves from religious conceptions. Bertrand Russell, in his famous sceptical essay, 'The Free Man's Worship' (1902), said that man, on recognizing that there is no God, should stand

proudly defiant of the irresistible forces that tolerate, for a moment, his knowledge and his condemnation, to sustain alone, a weary but unyielding Atlas, the world that his own ideals have fashioned despite the trampling march of unconscious power. [28]

An unyielding Atlas 'proudly defiant of the irresistible forces' and of 'the trampling march of unconscious power' ... The sense of heroic defiance depends on a sense of a vast foe to be heroically defied. The notion of the non-human (neutral) is being seductively confused with the notion of the inhuman (cruel). Later, Albert Camus, in 'The Myth of Sisyphus' (1943), commended his Sisyphus as one who scorns and defies those who have condemned him – the gods who, according to the essay, are non-existent. From thinking of the universe as non-human, neutral to man, it is easy to slide into the thought that the universe in its very neutrality is alien to man (who was once taught that anthropomorphic power beheld him), and thus to the thought that the universe, being so alien, is positively hostile to man – and finally to the thought that man is eminently courageous to defy so powerful a foe. A consolation lies in the way in which these shifts once again anthropomorphize the universe and permit the suffering individual to be seen as a heroic (if tragic) figure who defies overwhelming force.

Scepticism, then, may still retain some configurations of religious thought; and, in a society where institutional religion remains potent, the sceptic may revert guiltily to the arms of faith. As Hardy says in *Jude*: 'affliction makes opposing forces loom anthropomorphous'. Sue, in her bereavement, gains 'a sense of Jude and herself fleeing from a persecutor'.[29] She has sought to be intellectually liberated, but her suffering convinces her that a wrathful God is punishing her for her sins, and she undergoes an appalling penance. (Hardy was fond of quoting Gloucester's lines in *King Lear*: 'As flies to wanton boys are we to the gods: / They kill us for their sport'; and he noted that Lear himself was formerly the King of Wessex.)[30] So, though Hardy could diagnose belief in an actively cruel deity as a psychological malaise induced by suffering, such a belief sometimes loomed large in his own imagination. In *The Return of the Native*, Eustacia Vye (whose stance of Promethean defiance anticipates the stance advocated by Russell and Camus) is bitterly aware of 'the cruel satires that Fate loves to indulge in'; she places the blame upon 'some indistinct, colossal Prince of the World', and cries: 'O, how hard it is of Heaven to devise such tortures for me, who have done no harm to Heaven at all!' The narrator remarks that if she could have taken a detached view, she would have realized 'what a sport for Heaven this woman Eustacia was'.[31] Most significantly of all, the plot-structures of Hardy's major novels (particularly *Tess* and *Jude*), with their notorious coincidences and ruthless ironies, may seem to imply less the non-existence of God than the existence of a deity actively hostile to the sensitive, idealistic and well-meaning: a 'President of the Immortals' who indeed enjoys cruel sport. The idea which most commanded Hardy's intellectual and imaginative assent, however, was more sophisticated than this.

We are told that in those youthful days 'when her intellect scintillated like a star', Sue Bridehead had held

that the First Cause worked automatically like a somnambulist, and not reflectively like a sage; that at the framing of the terrestrial conditions there seemed never to have been contemplated such a development of emotional perceptiveness among the creatures subject to those conditions as that reached by thinking and educated humanity.[32]

These ideas are not Sue's only; they were ideas long held by Hardy. He formulated and re-formulated them in his notebooks over many years; they were versified in such poems as 'God's Funeral', 'The Sleep-Worker', 'New Year's Eve' and 'God's Education'; and they gained their fullest literary expression in his *The Dynasts*. His preoccupation with evolution suggested to him a 'First Cause' or 'Creative Will' which created blindly, so that human beings have exceeded in awareness their creator and the scheme of things; humans are conscious, sensitive and reflective amid an unconscious, insensitive and unreflective cosmos. When the 1914–18 war began, Hardy noted that events strengthened his notion 'that the never-ending push of the Universe was an unpurposive and irresponsible groping in the direction of the least resistance'.[33] Certainly, that war shed an ironic light on the hope expressed at the end of *The Dynasts*, that the Creative Will, which for so long 'mould[s] numbly / As in a dream', may eventually evolve into consciousness, realize what a mess it has made so far, and atone by reforming the creation: 'Consciousness the Will informing, till it fashion all things fair!'[34] As Darwin had shown reflective awareness dawning in humans after aeons of evolution, so Hardy envisaged a tardy growth of awareness in the creative force. He deemed this 'evolutionary meliorism' an original idea: 'my own idea solely'.[35] It may partly echo the Hegelian conception of a spirit of history which at last reaches a point of self-awareness, or Schopenhauer's belief in a life-force (*'der Wille'*) which engenders its opponent, critical awareness; Aeschylus' *Oresteia* showed Zeus evolving from obscure destructiveness to rational constructiveness; and Shelley's *Prometheus Unbound* envisaged the benign transformation of a hitherto oppressive cosmos. Nevertheless, the combination of topical evolutionary theories with Hardy's own brooding preoccupation with the shortcomings of any creator deemed anthropomorphic would have sufficed to suggest the idea. It remains illogical. To suppose that the forces of gravity or entropy should develop a brain is absurd enough; to suppose that the totality of forces in the universe should develop a conscious identity of its own is even more absurd. Only the anthropomorphic habit of mind, the perennial desire to humanize the non-human environment, lends it a specious plausibility.

When Sue thinks that the First Cause 'worked automatically, like a somnambulist', she manifests the considerable influence on Hardy of the conception of somnambulism. The combined notions of somnambulism (sleepwalking or automatism) and hypnotism had commanded interest from the time of Friedrich Anton Mesmer (1734–1815), exponent of 'Mesmerism' or 'animal magnetism' – hypnotism. Hardy knew Schopenhauer's *Two Essays*, which cited 'animal magnetism' as further evidence that 'the will [is] the kernel of Nature'.[36] Literary works by E. T. A. Hoffmann, Wilkie Collins, Charles Dickens and August Strindberg (particularly the Strindberg of *The Father* and *Miss Julie*) had all exploited the related ideas of automatic, involuntary or wilfully imposed activity; and the possibilities were still being exploited as late as 1919, in Robert Wiene's classic expressionist film, *The Cabinet of Dr Caligari*, and even 1926, in Fritz Lang's futuristic *Metropolis*. Although frequently the ideas were exploited in a trivializing, sensationalistic manner, they could sometimes be linked to a widespread fear created by the Victorian confusion of causality with determinism. Given that science was proving so adept at revealing the causal laws operating within diverse phenomena, the sense that natural activities were *subject* to such laws often led to the illogical but understandable inference that natural activities were *determined* by them; in which case, it appeared that humans were not free agents but puppets of causality. (This inference confused explanatory models with determining forces, and mistook logical entailment for physical compulsion.) Dostoyevsky's 'Underground Man' notes that men appear to be 'the keys of a piano, which the laws of nature threaten to control so completely'; T. H. Huxley declared, 'We are conscious automata'; and Conrad would speak of 'the whole scheme of things of which we form a helpless part'.[37]

In 1882 Hardy contemplated writing 'a history of human automatism, or impulsion' (which emerged as *The Dynasts*).[38] Occasionally his characters are depicted as resembling automata: thus, in *The Return of the Native*, Johnny Nunsuch 'seemed a mere automaton, galvanized into moving and speaking by the wayward Eustacia's will', and Mrs Yeobright finally behaves like 'one in a mesmeric sleep'.[39] Hardy was capable, moreover, of imagining that free will was almost entirely an illusion. In our actions, we generally serve the creative force or 'Great Will'; but

whenever it happens that all the rest of the Great Will is in equilibrium the minute portion called one person's will is free, just as a performer's fingers are free to go on playing the pianoforte of themselves when he talks or thinks of something else and the head does not rule them.[40]

Even more gloomy, perhaps, is Hardy's idea that the 'Great Will' itself is a mere somnambulist or 'Sleep-Worker', creating because it must, and thus creating individuals who tragically awaken into awareness of the cruelties of the cosmos in which, gratuitously and senselessly, they perforce exist.[41] Other sceptics shared, in varying degrees, this daunting view: it is bitterly rehearsed in the correspondence of Conrad, Cunninghame Graham and Edward Garnett during the 1890s, and their inheritors included Sartre, Camus and Beckett. Its presence is pervasive in Hardy's major novels; and, though it finds most explicit elaboration in the verse of *The Dynasts*, it gains its most incisive expression in *Jude*.

In 1890, Hardy had written: 'I have been looking for God 50 years, and I think that if he had existed I should have discovered him.'[42] On his deathbed, on 11 January 1928, this was the scene:

As it grew dusk, after a long musing silence, he asked his wife to repeat to him a verse from the *Rubáiyát of Omar Khayyám*, beginning

Oh, Thou, who man of baser Earth –

She took his copy of this work from his bedside and read to him:

Oh, Thou, who man of baser Earth didst make,
And ev'n with Paradise devise the Snake:

For all the Sin wherewith the Face of Man
Is blacken'd – Man's forgiveness give – and take![43]

It was a fine and courageous ending to his lifelong reflections on religion. From the early religious enthusiasm which had made him wish to be a clergyman, through the gradual waning of faith, via various combinations of scepticism, agnosticism, atheism, antitheism and evolutionary theology, his pilgrim's progress concluded with a defiant, sardonic and partly-antitheistic stanza. Fitzgerald's version of the *Rubáiyát* expressed the illogical but historically understandable view that the Creator was both non-existent (other than as a projection of the erring human imagination) and existent but hostile or uncaring: an ambivalence pervasive in Hardy's poetry and prose.

Hardy had declared: 'Pessimism . . . . . is, in brief, playing the sure game. You cannot lose at it; you may gain. It is the only view of life in which you can never be disappointed.'[44] The narrator of *Tess* refers to 'the chronic melancholy which is taking hold of the civilized races with the decline of belief in a beneficent Power'.[45] One of the most obvious causes of the pessimism which is so marked a feature of the late Victorian cultural climate was the loss of religious belief. Matthew Arnold, in 'Dover Beach', spoke of the 'melancholy, long, withdrawing roar' of the sea of faith. Scientific discoveries in geology, physics and biology, the evident progress attained by empirical procedures, and new historical analyses of the various books of the Bible: all these had served to erode religious convictions. *Essays and Reviews* (1860), by seven liberal churchmen, caused scandal by its sophisticated analyses of the Bible's implausibilities and archaic inconsistency with recent knowledge. Sue reflects the new sceptical, critical spirit when she derides the traditional marginal glosses of the Song of Solomon: glosses designed to tame as pious allegory the patent eroticism of the original verses.[46] Nevertheless, the pervasive power of the church and of religious reference-points for conduct remained strong.

When Hardy described himself as 'churchy', he meant not only that he had long been preoccupied with religious matters, not only that he could relate present problems readily to biblical texts (Job, Corinthians, Numbers, Judges, Ecclesiastes, the Song of Solomon, Revelation and the Gospels being cited in *Jude*), but also that all his life he liked to attend church services and was profoundly moved by particular hymns and anthems. There was a strong aesthetic element here, and also a form of cultural nostalgia for a church with which his father, grandfather and their friends, as musicians of the 'quire', had for so long been associated. Hardy also entertained the apparently illogical hope that the Anglican Church might so dilute its doctrines, purging them of 'preternatural assumptions', as to open its gates to agnostics.[47] Tennyson had written:

> There lives more faith in honest doubt,
> Believe me, than in half the creeds.[48]

Hardy's hope for a church of 'honest doubt' has been almost fulfilled in the late twentieth century as the Anglican Church successively diluted its doctrines. Sue shares Hardy's nostalgia and his love of Swinburne when she says:

To be sure, at times one couldn't help having a sneaking liking for the traditions of the old faith . . . . .; but when I was in my saddest, rightest mind I always felt, 'O ghastly glories of saints, dead limbs of gibbeted Gods!'[49]

In the suffering heroes of the Old and New Testaments – Job, Samson and Jesus (particularly the Jesus who said, 'My God, my God, why hast thou forsaken me?')[50] – Hardy found reference-points and exemplars for aspects of the characterization of Jude. Indeed, *Jude the Obscure* can be regarded as a *Pilgrim's Progress* rewritten by a sceptic: a progress not towards salvation but towards the nirvana of death, under heavens that seem sometimes empty and sometimes the stronghold of a hostile or uncaring force. To Hardy's readiness to imagine the Creator as nonexistent, as deceased, as a poignant delusion, as existent but cruel, and as a blundering somnambulist, we may trace the most radical tensions and ambivalences of that novel. A lapsed Christian is more likely to appreciate its bitter power than is a fully secular reader; because *Jude the Obscure*, the story of an orphan, is a lament for the metaphysically orphaned, for all those abandoned by a mortally mythical Father.

3.3 Hebraism and Hellenism

In *Culture and Anarchy* (1869) Matthew Arnold influentially analysed culture in terms of 'Hebraism' and 'Hellenism'. 'The governing idea of Hellenism is *spontaneity of consciousness*; that of Hebraism, *strictness of conscience*.'[51] Hebraism is the religious tradition, with its emphasis on sin and on the importance of virtuous conduct in the world; Hellenism is the tradition of 'sweetness and light', the appreciation of beauty, and the desire to let 'a free play of thought live and flow around all our activity'.[52] He suggested that at his time, in the nineteenth century, Hebraism was all too dominant and needed to be tempered by a

Hellenistic openness to life. Admittedly, when Arnold gave illustrations of his own 'sweetness and light' in considering political topics, he proved to be sourly conventional in his middle-class fear of the masses: '[M]onster processions in the streets and forcible irruptions into the parks, even in professed support of this good design [the abolition of the slave-trade], ought to be unflinchingly forbidden and repressed . . . . .'[53] Nevertheless, Arnold was at least helping to extend the challenge which had been made more incisively and intelligently by J. S. Mill in *On Liberty* (1859): the challenge to a dominant religious ideology by liberal, sceptical thought which sought to extend individual liberties. Speaking of Christianity, Mill declared:

Its ideal is negative rather than positive; . . . . . in its precepts (as has been well said) 'thou shalt not' predominates unduly over 'thou shalt'. In its horror of sensuality, it made an idol of asceticism, which has been gradually compromised away into one of legality. It holds out the hope of heaven and the threat of hell, as the appointed and appropriate motives to a virtuous life: in this falling far below the best of the ancients . . . . . [I]n the morality of private life, whatever exists of magnanimity, high-mindedness, personal dignity, even the sense of honour, is derived from the purely human, not the religious part of our education . . . . .[54]

The person who is guided by convention and tradition instead of thinking for himself or herself 'has no need of any other faculty than the ape-like one of imitation', asserted Mill; and, in *Jude the Obscure*, Sue fervently repeats his assertion to the hapless Phillotson.[55]

The protest against Hebraism gained fervently lyrical expression in the poems of Swinburne, most notoriously in his 'Hymn to Proserpine', a dramatic monologue which purported to be the lament of a Roman at the proclamation of Christianity but which was clearly a covert protest at the repressive climate of Victorianism:

Wilt thou yet take all, Galilean? but these thou shalt not take,
The laurel, the palms and the paean, the breasts of the nymphs in the brake
. . . . .
Thou hast conquered, O pale Galilean; the world has grown grey from thy breath;
We have drunk on things Lethean, and fed on the fullness of death.[56]

In his 'Hymn of Man', Swinburne even declared the death of God:

Thou art smitten, thou God, thou art smitten; thy death is upon thee, O Lord.
And the love-song of earth as thou diest resounds through the wind of her wings –
Glory to Man in the highest! for Man is the master of things.[57]

Swinburne's protests derived from the Romanticism of Blake and Shelley, in which a repressive God was denounced as a tyrant fettering human liberty and spontaneity; and Shelley had been influenced by the scepticism of eighteenth-century rationalists, notably Voltaire, Hume and Gibbon, in addition to William Godwin (whose *Enquiry Concerning Political Justice* had appeared in 1793). In turn, Swinburne's poetry contributed strongly to the Aesthetic Movement of the late nineteenth century. Walter Pater, echoed by his disciple and popularizer Oscar Wilde, repeatedly advocated a return to Hellenic values, associated with hedonistic liberty (including homosexuality) and the cultivation of the senses; and Pater's works were studied by Hardy, who knew him personally.[58]

Thomas Hardy had read Arnold's *Culture and Anarchy*; J. S. Mill was one of his cultural heroes; Shelley and Swinburne were among his favourite poets; and he relished the scepticism of Gibbon. All these authors are cited in *Jude the Obscure*; Gibbon, for instance, is epitomized as 'the smoothly shaven historian so ironically civil to Christianity'.[59] (In his journal, Hardy noted with some pride that the furore occasioned by *Jude the Obscure* was the greatest since the publication of Swinburne's *Poems and Ballads* in 1866.)[60] Chapters II.ii, II.iii and II.iv of the novel set forth the contrast between Hellenism and Hebraism with an abrasive starkness utterly unlike the vague, bland diplomacy of Arnold's discussion.

At her workplace, Sue is obliged to toil in the service of Hebraism, painting Christian texts and slogans (e.g. 'Alleluja' – 'Praise Yahweh'); but her inner Hellenism is graphically shown by her purchase of the statuettes of Apollo and Venus. She sets them on her chest of drawers like tutelary deities while (in contrast to Jude's close study of the Bible) she reads first the sceptical Gibbon's chapters on Julian the Apostate, who renounced Christianity and reverted to paganism, and next Swinburne's 'Hymn to Proserpine' (the very line about the 'pale Galilean') – one associative link between the two works being that Julian provided the epigraph to the poem. When the aptly named Miss Fontover, the abbess-like guardian of the ecclesiastical workplace, inquires which statuettes Sue has purchased, the reply is: 'St. Peter and St. – St. Mary Magdalen'. Eventually, Miss Fontover identifies and smashes the figures. Sue Bridehead's intellectual revolt against Hebraism is ironically contrasted with Jude's Christian preoccupations: while she reads Swinburne, he toils at Griesbach's New Testament, and fondly imagines that she, evidently devoted to 'A sweet, saintly, Christian business', might become for him 'an elevating power, a companion in Anglican worship'.

(He has outgrown the phase in which he knelt in pagan adoration of Diana, the moon-goddess, and Apollo.) Thus Sue's activities clearly symbolize the extent to which the Hellenism of the late Victorian age was a sign and symptom of ideological revolt against the repressiveness of established Christianity and of the associated moral codes and taboos. When she visits the exhibition of the model of Jerusalem, her comment to Phillotson is typically Hellenistic:

'I fancy we have had enough of Jerusalem,' she said, 'considering we are not descended from the Jews. There was nothing first-rate about the place, or people, after all – as there was about Athens, Rome, Alexandria, and other old cities.'

'But my dear girl, consider what it is to us!'

She was silent, for she was easily repressed . . . . . [61]

The comment 'easily repressed' does not seem generally true of Sue's sceptical freethinking; she delights in educating Jude in modern heresy, and the combination of her ideas and adverse circumstances leads him towards scepticism. Of course, as Hardy designed, Hebraism then achieves a cruel victory over her Hellenism when, shattered by the deaths of the children, she is overtaken by religious guilt and returns to Phillotson. What is illustrated there, graphically and almost melodramatically, is the familiar cultural fact that a sustained emancipation of outlook proves exceptionally difficult when a dominant repressive ideology remains pervasive and officially authoritative, and when religious modes of thought are so ubiquitous that even the 'liberated' individual may still be infiltrated by notions of supernatural punishment for 'sin'. Sue herself becomes another 'apostate': a martyr, like so many other people in real life, to the ideological divisions of her era.

Matthew Arnold's essay 'Heine' (noted by Hardy) had declared that 'the modern spirit' is in revolt against 'accredited dogmas, systems, rules':

The modern spirit is now awake almost everywhere; the sense of want of correspondence between the forms of modern Europe and its spirit, between the new wine of the eighteenth and nineteenth centuries, and the old bottles of the eleventh and twelfth centuries, or even of the sixteenth and seventeenth, almost every one now perceives . . . . .

The emancipated Sue repeats Arnold's image when she remarks:

[I]ntellect at Christminster is new wine in old bottles. The mediævalism of Christminster must go, be sloughed off, or Christminster itself will have to go. [62]

Accordingly, she protests against 'the social moulds' of civilization which fail to fit 'our actual shapes'; and here she echoes a Hellenistic notion (influenced by Fourier's Utopianism) which Hardy had expressed in a letter of 1893:

I consider a social system based on individual spontaneity to promise better for happiness than a curbed and uniform one under which all temperaments are bound to shape themselves to a single pattern of living.[63]

'It is doubtful', comments Hardy drily, 'if this Utopian scheme possessed Hardy's fancy for any long time'. Oscar Wilde's remarks are apposite:

The new Individualism is the new Hellenism.

A map of the world that does not include Utopia is not worth even glancing at . . . . .[64]

In the case of Sue in *Jude the Obscure*, harsh Hebraism triumphs over the Utopian hopes of the new Hellenism.

3.4 The 'New Woman'

In the 1912 'Postscript' to the original 1895 'Preface' of *Jude*, Hardy noted:

After the issue of *Jude the Obscure* as a serial story in Germany, an experienced reviewer of that country informed the writer that Sue Bridehead, the heroine, was the first delineation in fiction of the woman who was coming into notice in her thousands every year – the woman of the feminist movement – the slight, pale 'bachelor' girl – the intellectualized, emancipated bundle of nerves that modern conditions were producing, mainly in cities as yet; who does not recognize the necessity for most of her sex to follow marriage as a profession, and boast themselves as superior people because they are licensed to be loved on the premises. The regret of this critic was that the portrait of the newcomer had been left to be drawn by a man, and was not done by one of her own sex, who would never have allowed her to break down at the end.[65]

The German reviewer did not, apparently, read very widely. The characterization of Sue was not the 'first delineation' but was already part of a tradition: the tradition of representation of the 'New Woman', the proto-feminist, the young woman who is educated, intelligent, emancipated in ideas and in morality, and who is resistant to the conventional notion that marriage and maternity should be the goal of any normal female's progress.

The Romantic Movement's call for the liberation of the enslaved, oppressed and exploited, whether the blacks, the underpaid workers, or the small nations annexed by the larger, had inevitably re-echoed as a call for the liberation of women. The great pioneering feminist of the late eighteenth century, Mary Wollstonecraft (wife of William Godwin and mother of Mary Shelley), lamented the fact that the education of females was sadly inferior to that of males and that so many women's lives were stunted by the dominance of the 'wife-and-mother' stereotype. Those ideas, expounded in *A Vindication of the Rights of Woman* (1792), were influentially revived by J. S. Mill's *The Subjection of Women* (1869). He opposed the legal subjection of women to men, saying that 'it ought to be replaced by a principle of perfect equality, admitting no power or privilege on the one side, nor disability on the other'. He continued:

What is now called the nature of women is an eminently artificial thing – the result of forced repression in some directions, unnatural stimulation in others . . . . .

[N]o one can safely pronounce that if women's nature were left to choose its direction as freely as men's . . . . . there would be any material difference, or perhaps any difference at all, in the character and capacities which would unfold themselves.[66]

The Victorian authorities were zealous in promoting education. This zeal stemmed partly from a desire to tame the masses and to control an expanding electorate by imbuing them with bourgeois values. As Mill noted in his *Subjection of Women*, already women were organized to demand equality of opportunity in education and in admission to the professions. In London, Queen's College and Bedford College admitted women in 1848 and 1849 respectively, producing the first generation of highly qualified women teachers. Soon women entered the North London Collegiate (1850), Cheltenham Ladies' College (1854) and Girton, Cambridge (1869). Nurses, too, were now given professional training. Meanwhile, expanding businesses needed competent clerks: 'the census returns of 1861 and 1871 show no female clerks at all; by 1881 there were nearly 6000 and by 1891 the number had almost trebled to 17,859 – the Typewriter Girl had arrived.'[67] The greater educational opportunities for women naturally strengthened their claims to the electoral franchise; but in 1870 their Suffrage Bill was blocked by Parliament. In 1895 (when Hardy's novel appeared) more than half the Members of Parliament were, in theory, supporters of the principle of women's suffrage; though, in the event, not until 1918 did British women (over the age of thirty) gain the vote.

During the nineteenth century the lot of wives also gained slow improvements. Before 1857, divorce was costly and difficult, requiring an Act of Parliament. The Matrimonial Causes Act in that year made divorce easier, though there remained the assumption that women should be sexually more restrained than men. A husband could sue for divorce on the grounds of his wife's adultery, but a wife could sue only if her husband had been guilty of incestuous adultery, rape, sodomy, bestiality, adultery coupled with cruelty, or adultery coupled with desertion. At least the Married Women's Property Acts of 1870 and 1882 gave the woman a legal right to retain her own property instead of surrendering it to her husband.

In 1794 William Blake had condemned 'the Marriage hearse';[68] and later Shelley strongly advocated free love, claiming that it was absurd that marriage should shackle together individuals whose emotions would naturally change in course of time. (Inconsistently, Shelley became married, twice.) The more radical novels of the nineteenth century often voiced the claims of the woman to equality with men, and deplored the fetters of marriage to an unworthy husband. Charlotte Brontë's Jane Eyre protests that 'women feel just as men feel; they need exercise for their faculties, and a field for their efforts as much as their brothers do'.[69] Anne Brontë's *The Tenant of Wildfell Hall* portrayed a woman who, married to a dissolute alcoholic, eventually leaves him, taking her son with her. George Eliot, too, gave sympathetic portrayals of women striving for independence yet often subjugated within marriage; none of her heroines, however, was as emancipated as George Eliot herself, who, while successfully pursuing a literary career, lived openly with a married man (G. H. Lewes) until his death. The 'woman question' gained new impetus from the *succès de scandale* of Ibsen's play *A Doll's House* (1879, but first performed in London in 1889). In the early 1890s, the 'New Woman' appeared in plays by Shaw (particularly *Mrs Warren's Profession*, 1894) and in numerous novels and tales, notably Sarah Grand's *The Heavenly Twins* (1893), *Keynotes* (1893) by 'George Egerton' (Mary Clairmonte), Mona Caird's *The Daughters of Danaus* (1894) and Grant Allen's *The Woman Who Did* (1895). Repeatedly, the fictional 'New Woman' is portrayed as intelligent, lively, articulately forthright, capable of pursuing her own career, sexually daring (whether in seductive action or defiant abstinence), and resistant to the conventional claims of marriage. In *Mrs Warren's Profession*, Vivie Warren, Cambridge educated, successfully wards off her suitors and becomes devoted to her career as an actuarist. More usually, though, the New Woman's revolt ends either tragically or in conformity.

Herminia, the heroine of *The Woman Who Did*, eventually commits suicide; Gypsy of *Keynotes* succumbs to the claims of maternity; Evadne, in *The Heavenly Twins*, emerges from a mental breakdown to acquiesce in a second marriage and motherhood.

Hardy's heroines often display a lively degree of independence: Cytherea, Fancy Day, Ethelberta, Bathsheba and Tess all earn their own livings. Though they are sexually attractive, repeatedly this asset resembles a liability: they are pursued and sometimes harassed by their impatient or reproachful suitors. This pattern is maintained in Sue Bridehead, who offers a clear instance of new enlightenment linked to educational opportunity. She is naturally intelligent and interested in ideas; since leaving school she has been further educated by contact with the student at London with whom she (to his frustration) lived in celibate companionship; before meeting Jude, she has taught for two years in the city; and, after meeting Phillotson, she wins a Queen's scholarship to attend the Training College at Melchester and qualify fully for a career as a teacher. While Jude's advance towards the University is inexorably checked, her more modest educational ambition gains, at first, easy fulfilment. What eventually ends her progress in the career is the social stigma of her elopement with Jude. When initially married to Phillotson, she makes clear her revulsion from sexual union with him; and, even when Phillotson has divorced her, she recoils from the prospect of marriage to Jude, feeling that it would blight their life, and maintains for a long time her celibate state. Hardy is highly ambivalent in his presentation of Jude's desire for her: part of the time the narrative shows keen sympathy with Jude's sexual frustration and his tantalization by Sue's mixture of the seductive and the resistant; part of the time it sympathizes with Sue's endeavour to preserve an integrity unviolated by the claims of the flesh.

Jude the Obscure depicts divorce as easily obtainable (provided that the divorced spouse is a female presumed guilty of adultery), and particularly easy for ordinary people. Jude remarks that 'obscure people' can be dealt with 'in a rough and ready fashion', whereas 'patented nobilities' would have had 'infinite trouble'.[70] Nevertheless, Hardy depicts marriage as a snare, and maintains a satiric animus against the institution of wedlock. For instance, we are told that their landlord suspects, on seeing Arabella kiss Jude, that they may be living in sin:

and he was about to give them notice to quit, till by chance overhearing her one night haranguing Jude in rattling terms, and ultimately flinging a shoe at his head, he recognized the note of ordinary wedlock; and concluding that they must be respectable, said no more.[71]

In *Tess of the d'Urbervilles* Hardy had powerfully condemned the double standard whereby women are expected to preserve a 'purity' which men can readily forfeit; and in *Jude the Obscure* he indicts marriage in general (as Blake and Shelley had done) for imposing a nominal permanence on variable emotions and particularly for subjecting the woman to the sexual demands of the man.

Gail Cunningham has rightly noted some elements of conventionality in the workings of the plot:

Sue's career follows a pattern made familiar by the New Woman writers: theoretically emancipated to start with, she suddenly and almost inexplicably marries the wrong man, makes an initially successful bid for freedom and then collapses into crushing conformity. This is an exact parallel to the sequence of Hadria's life in *The Daughters of Danaus* and bears general similarity to the plots of other New Woman novels. Almost all New Woman heroines break down at the end, most go through some period of nervous prostration if not madness, and both Evadne and Hadria anticipate Sue in turning back to the Church in their defeat.[72]

Even Sue's elusive variability was a familiar characteristic. Gypsy in *Keynotes* (studied by Hardy) says of women:

'At heart we care nothing for laws, nothing for systems . . . . . Perhaps many of our seeming contradictions are only the outward evidences of inward chafing . . . . . A woman must beware of speaking the truth to a man; he loves her the less for it. It is the elusive spirit in her that he divines but cannot seize, that fascinates and keeps him.'[73]

A remarkably radical comment is offered by the astute Professor Theobald in *Daughters of Danaus*:

'It is the fashion, I know . . . . . to regard woman as an enigma . . . . . I believe that this is a mistake. Woman is an enigma, certainly, because she is human, but that ends it. Her conditions have tended to develop in her the power of dissimulation, and the histrionic quality, just as the peaceful ilex learns to put forth thorns if you expose it to the attacks of devouring cattle . . . . . Let a man's subsistence and career be subject to the same powers and chances as the success of a woman's life now hangs on, and see whether he too does not become a histrionic enigma.'[74]

The elusiveness, so marked in Sue, is partly an expression of the New Woman's divided responses to sexuality: in reality, some emancipated women (like Mona Caird and Olive Schreiner) advocated free sexual union, while others (like Kathlyn Oliver and Christabel Pankhurst) advocated rigorous sexual abstinence.[75]

It appears, then, that Hardy was not as original as his 'Postscript'

implied, for the New Woman was already a well-represented phenomenon when the book of *Jude* appeared in 1895. George Bernard Shaw
claimed that discussion of the New Woman was at its height in 1893,
and in 1896 the *Saturday Review* declared that this literary topic had
expired a year previously and that there was already a reaction against
it.[76] The ambivalence of the treatment of Sue's revolt – a revolt which,
though sympathetically depicted, is also shown to meet its nemesis –
was certainly a common ambivalence in literature of the time. The
German reviewer who complained that a female novelist 'would never
have allowed her to break down at the end' was clearly wrong, for
females like Mona Caird, George Egerton and Sarah Grand had described such breakdowns, whereas male playwrights (Ibsen and Bernard
Shaw)[77] had shown revolts successfully carried out. Given the extent of
the oppressive and repressive forces in society and in the ideology of
the time, there may well have been plenty of real-life counterparts to
the defeated and broken New Women; a century later, the battle for
women's equality is still being fought, and full victory remains elusive.

In *Jude the Obscure*, the author's allegiances veer markedly between, on
the one side, sympathy for the independently minded young woman who
seeks to elude stereotyping and, on the other, endorsement of some
traditional stereotypes. The biography cites Hardy's remark that a woman
is 'one of the sex that makes up for lack of justice by excess of generosity',
which echoes the narrator's comments that Sue is 'essentially large-
minded and generous on reflection, despite a previous exercise of those
narrow womanly humours on impulse that were necessary to give her
sex'.[78] Nevertheless, when *Jude the Obscure* is compared with other novels
of that time which depict the New Woman, Hardy's novel is generally
more vivid, intense and moving than they are. Hardy's shifts between the
general and the particular, between theoretical debate and the concretely
realized details of life, and his strongly dialectical imagination which
repeatedly generates ironic contrasts and juxtapositions – all these give
Sue a stronger reality than the fictional New Woman customarily acquires.
Hardy lent his powerful influence to an enduring cause. The New Woman
of the 1890s was the mother of the militant suffragists of the period 1906–
14; and their descendants today remain numerous and active.

3.5 The Tragic Tradition; Naturalism; Fielding

In the 1895 'Preface', Hardy refers to *Jude the Obscure* as a novel which
attempts 'to point . . . . . the tragedy of unfulfilled aims'; and, in the
1912 'Postscript', he says:

My opinion at that time, if I remember rightly, was what it is now, that a marriage should be dissolvable as soon as it becomes a cruelty to either of the parties – being then essentially and morally no marriage – and it seemed a good foundation for the fable of a tragedy, told for its own sake as a presentation of particulars containing a good deal that was universal, and not without a hope that certain cathartic, Aristotelian qualities might be found therein.[79]

His phrasing in the last few lines invokes the famous discussion of tragedy in Aristotle's *Poetics*. Aristotle had emphasized the prime importance of plot, or 'fable', among the components of a tragic drama, and had established the doctrine that the power of tragic poetry lies in its reconciliation of the particular and the universal; the poet must not merely offer vivid imitations but must reveal the general laws underlying human conduct. Thus 'poetry is something more philosophical and more worthy of serious attention than history; for while poetry is concerned with universal truths, history treats of particular facts.'[80] Hardy also invokes Aristotle's celebrated theory of 'catharsis' (or 'purgation'). Plato, in *The Republic*, had advocated censorship of literature, arguing that the passions and crimes depicted in fiction might infect the audience; therefore Aristotle, to defend literature against this Platonic accusation, offered the counter-argument that, far from filling the audience with dangerous feelings, literature actually drains us of such feelings. Tragedy, he said, uses pity and fear to bring about 'the purgation of such emotions'; pity and fear are elicited and purged from us.[81]

There is no doubt that, when writing some of his novels, Hardy had classical tragedies in mind; and, as we have seen, he long cherished the idea that his masterwork would be the verse-drama which emerged as *The Dynasts* – an idea which may have been prompted by his reading of Aeschylus' *The Oresteia*, and perhaps by Shelley's *Prometheus Unbound*. As a counterpart to the classical tragic chorus of citizens or servants, *The Dynasts* employs various choric groups ('Chorus of the Years', 'Chorus of the Pities', etc.), and his novels often include a commentary by groups of rustic figures. Repeatedly, Hardy sought to relate his protagonists to classical precedents. In *The Return of the Native*, Eustacia is linked to Nausicaa, Clym to Prometheus. Aeschylus, the most august of Greek tragedians, is explicitly invoked at the close of *Tess of the d'Urbervilles*. In *Jude the Obscure*, both Jude and Sue are well-versed in classic tragedies: Jude quotes Sophocles' *Antigone* and Aeschylus' *Agamemnon*; and, tellingly, Sue remarks of their ancestral misfortunes, 'It makes me feel as if a tragic doom overhung our family, as it did the house of Atreus.'[82] In Greek drama, one distinctive kind of motivation is what might be termed 'hereditary impulsion': in the present action, certain characters perform certain destructive deeds because they have inherited the ancestral tendency to destruction. Thus, in *The Oresteia*, the house of Atreus is accursed because, long ago, Tantalus killed his son Pelops and served him as a banquet for the gods. Tantalus' descendants, the brothers Atreus and Thyestes, fall to dissension; Atreus murders two of Thyestes' sons and serves them in a banquet for their father; a surviving son, Aegisthus, conspires with Clytemnestra to kill Atreus' son, Agamemnon; and eventually both Clytemnestra and Aegisthus are slain by Agamemnon's heir, Orestes.

In *Jude the Obscure*, the milder counterpart to such 'hereditary impulsion' is the curse which appears to befall marriages in the Fawley family. As Hardy put it, the novel concerns 'the tragic issues of two bad marriages, owing in the main to a doom or curse of hereditary temperament peculiar to the family of the parties'.[83] Jude's great-aunt Drusilla urges him not to make contact with his cousin Sue, not merely because sexual relationships between first cousins entail genetic risks, but largely because his ancestry would double the chance of a disastrous marriage: '[I]n a family like his own where marriage usually meant a tragic sadness, marriage with a blood-relation would duplicate the adverse conditions, and a tragic sadness might be intensified to a tragic horror.'[84] (The insistent repetition of the adjective 'tragic' makes clear Hardy's wish to invoke ancient precedent.) Sue has been warned by her father that marriage 'always ended badly for us Fawleys'. Her parents quarrelled and separated; the same misfortune befell Jude's parents, his mother drowning herself after the estrangement. On the eve of the intended marriage of Jude and Sue, Mrs Edlin tells them the gloomy and melodramatic tale of their common ancestor, a man whose wife had run away from him with their child, and who, breaking into her house when the child had died ('to steal the coffin away'), had been arrested and hanged for burglary; 'his wife went mad after he was dead'. These predictions of misfortune in marriage are obviously fulfilled: not only are the respective marriages of Sue and Jude disastrous, but also, when they attempt to live together as man and wife (although formally unmarried), the children perish and they separate. Jude's early death is partly a consequence of the estrangement.

At least, in Aeschylus' *Oresteia*, the cycle of dynastic disasters is eventually terminated harmoniously with the institution of civilized justice at Athens; Orestes is acquitted, and the tragic sequence ends in general rejoicing: humans and gods are constructively reconciled after the many dark and tormented years. Hardy, however, while attempting to invest his narrative with a sense of tragic doom and foreboding, concludes the story of Jude and Sue in bitter negativity. D. H. Lawrence once remarked, 'Tragedy ought really to be a great kick at misery';[85] to some commentators, Hardy has made *Jude the Obscure* a merely pessimistic work, therefore, and not a tragedy. What is evident is that the text's stress on the 'doomed marriages of the Fawleys' generates another marked tension in the work's ideas. Part of the time, Hardy argues that the relationship of Jude and Sue was blighted because social conditions were wrong for them: they were 'ahead of their times', and too enlightened for their own era. Against this, however, he deploys the notion that *no* times would have been right for them, since their familial inheritance has imparted to their very genes the likelihood of failure and unhappiness. Thus, Hardy the social reformer is combated by Hardy the would-be tragedian, seeking to offer a modern equivalent to the destinal forces of classical drama. As in some Modernist works, the result may resemble a partly parodic or ironically debased version of the august predecessor.

The idea that the scientific principle of heredity offered modern writers a convenient counterpart to the ancient sense of the doomed family was, of course, exploited in the nineteenth century by the so-called 'Naturalist' writers. Although 'Naturalism' is often used loosely as a mere synonym for 'Realism', it should, strictly, refer to principles developed by certain writers of the late nineteenth and early twentieth centuries. Strongly influenced by Darwinism and its popularizations, those writers sought to emphasize that man's life is part of the long-term evolutionary struggle and is governed by heredity and environment. Zola, Ibsen, Strindberg, Conrad, Crane, Dreiser and O'Neill shared, in varying degrees, this preoccupation. Joseph Conrad is strongly 'Naturalistic' in that episode of *The Secret Agent* (an episode influenced by Zola's *Thérèse Raquin*) in which Winnie Verloc stabs her husband to death: 'Into that plunging blow . . . . . Mrs Verloc had put all the inheritance of her immemorial and obscure descent, the simple ferocity of the age of caverns, and the unbalanced nervous fury of the age of bar-rooms.'[86] With almost schematic brevity, Naturalistic causality is thus supplied: heredity ('the simple ferocity of the age of caverns') and environment ('the unbalanced nervous fury of the age of bar-rooms') combine with fatal results.

In *Jude the Obscure*, Hardy shares, to a large extent, the preoccupations of Naturalism. An early reviewer commented: 'His sympathies are manifestly with the French naturalistic school of fiction.'[87] Not only does he emphasize the unfortunate heredity of the Fawleys, but also, on a much larger scale, he suggests the dire consequences for men of their biological inheritance; within them, nature and its sexual urges seem to challenge or subvert their idealism – hence that 'deadly war ..... between flesh and spirit'. Similarly, Hardy is zealous in establishing the various environmental pressures which both impel and frustrate his protagonists: educational opportunity is partly provided, educational fulfilment is largely denied; the scope for social mobility has increased (partly a consequence of the development of railways, of urbanization and of specializations in work), but the consequence is a deracination or alienation, a cultural and social rootlessness. In *Tess of the d'Urbervilles*, Tess experiences what is termed 'the ache of modernism', meaning, there, a vague sense of alienation and sombre foreboding; in *Jude*, that 'ache' is more specifically defined as 'the spirit of mental and social restlessness, that makes so many unhappy in these days'.[88] We may recall Conrad's claim that mankind is made tragic by its situation as a *conscious* 'part of the animal kingdom'; and writers as diverse as Edward Carpenter (author of *Civilization: Its Cause and Cure*), Walter Pater, Samuel Butler, Cunninghame Graham and the young Bertrand Russell lamented the melancholy vistas which resulted from the combination of scientific knowledge and civilized consciousness. If reflection revealed that man was descended from the primates and was not the child of God, more writers than Hardy might suspect that 'thought is a disease of flesh'.[89]

Émile Zola, whose English publisher had been jailed for publishing his 'immoral' fiction, was readily associated by Victorian reviewers with any English novelist who was deemed to be coarse or bold in depicting humans as 'part of the animal kingdom'. One reviewer of *Jude*, remarking that Zola's novels 'disgust rather than allure', declared: 'Mr. Hardy has long been creeping nearer and nearer to the fruit which has been so profitable to the French novelist .....'[90] While sharing with Zola's fiction a sexual frankness and a general interest in heredity and social pressures, *Jude the Obscure* is perhaps most Zolaesque in the physicality of the pig-killing scene; even so, the differences between the two writers greatly outweigh the similarities. Hardy is altogether less cumbrous, handling characterization more sensitively and displaying greater scenic and thematic mobility. And there was a potent English precedent for his morally incisive ironies. Hardy told Edmund Gosse:

As to the 'coarse' scenes with Arabella, the battle in the schoolroom, etc., the newspaper critics might, I thought, have sneered at them for their Fieldingism rather than for their Zolaism. I am read in Zola very little, but have felt akin locally to Fielding, so many of his scenes having been laid down this way, and his home near.[91]

Gosse, reviewing *Jude* in *Cosmopolis*, compared Hardy favourably with Zola and noted that he had surpassed Henry Fielding in sexual frankness;[92] but Hardy's letter suggests a larger connection with Fielding.

In the works of that eighteenth-century novelist, particularly *Tom Jones*, there was certainly ample precedent for a narrative in which a wandering hero succumbs to sexual temptation; loins subvert loyalties; and Arabella has an ancestor in the lusty Molly Seagrim. As in Hardy, Fielding's protagonists traverse a distinctly English terrain, largely rural ('Wessex'), partly urban, learning at first hand the hypocrisies of their supposedly Christian society. Fielding, like Hardy, sharply satirizes the uncharitable treatment of the humble and needy by the well-to-do; he, too, sardonically shows that there is one law for the rich and a harsher law for the poor; and he, too, heightens ironies by deploying coincidental meetings and coincidental failures to meet. As Hardy noted, the farcical 'battle in the schoolroom' (*Jude*, IV.vi) does indeed hold echoes (though distant and attenuated) of Fielding, notably of the slapstick comedy in Tom Jones's battle at the inn at Upton. The schematic moral ironies of Fielding's fiction, in which different characters respond in pointedly contrasting ways to the same moral dilemma, may have provided some precedent for the related schematic ironies of Hardy's. There are even analogies in stylistic range: Fielding ranges from mock-heroic rhetoric to vulgar vernacular dialogue; Hardy ranges from a rather pedantic style (with traces of mock-heroic) to coarse idiomatic repartee. The fact remains, of course, that the predominantly comic tone and providential tenor of *Tom Jones* contrast obviously with the predominantly bleak and pessimistic qualities of *Jude the Obscure*; a comedy of genial gusto has given way to a comedy of sardonic bitterness; and the wanderings of the picaresque hero have led him from festivity to fasting, from the homeland to the Waste Land.

Part 4 Contents of *Jude the Obscure*

4.1 The Texts

Jude the Obscure is a more protean work than we may at first recognize. Initially it was conceived as a short story. Hardy's journal for 28 April 1888 says: 'A short story of a young man – "who could not go to Oxford" – His struggles and ultimate failure. Suicide.'[1] The writing extended between 1890 and 1895. A manuscript of the resultant novel has survived, having been presented by the author to the Fitzwilliam Museum, Cambridge. This is incomplete and bears temporary alterations made solely for the first published version, the serial text; that serial differs significantly from the first book edition; and subsequently Hardy made various revisions for the book editions of 1903 and 1912.

The manuscript, which bears the title *Jude the Obscure* above a sequence of cancelled titles (*The Simpletons | Part First | Hearts Insurgent | The Dreamer*), lacks a number of pages dealing with sexual encounters. These had had to be drastically changed for serialization. Although otherwise the manuscript corresponds in the main to the first book text, it bears some alterations to adapt the narrative to the serial's bowdlerizations. Hardy's notes on pp. 1 and 52 of the MS emphasize that those alterations made for serial publication 'have no authority beyond'. In the early pages, various cancelled passages show that the author, who initially names the hero 'Jack' rather than 'Jude', intended his hero's interest in Christminster to be aroused by his knowledge that his cousin Sue was there, she having been adopted by the Provost of 'Cloister College'; and originally it was she, not Phillotson, who sent to the young lad the package of Latin grammar-books. For example, Jack's great-aunt originally said to him: 'Jack, Jack, why dont you go & get the Head of a College to adopt ee, as your cousin has done.' Hardy later substituted the following words: 'Jude, Jude, why didstn't go off with that schoolmaster of thine to Christminster or somewhere!' Other changes show Hardy going back over the pages to make insertions which initiate ironic sequences: thus Phillotson's early advice to Jude to 'be kind to animals and birds' was an insertion generated in retrospect from the farmer's chastisement of the kindly rook-scarer. Other changes refine the ironies: Hardy crossed out a reference to the old Marygreen church as 'the ancient temple of God' and substituted 'the ancient temple to the Christian divinities'. There were also retrospective thematic refinements: I noticed that originally the picture which, at the inn, looked down on Arabella and Jude showed 'Susannah & the Elders' (incidentally revealing why the book's heroine was named Sue), but Hardy substituted 'Samson & Delilah', so as to make a sardonic commentary on Arabella's seduction of the young hero. In short, the manuscript is a fine illustration of the evolutionary nature of the process of composition; its absent leaves mutely condemn Victorian bowdlerization; and its very presence in the Fitzwilliam makes an irony that Hardy had foreseen and invited by his donation, for now scholars enter this academic citadel to study these hallowed pages which tell the story of a studious man who failed to enter a university.

Serialization took place between December 1894 and November 1895. In the first instalment, the title was *The Simpletons*; in the second, it became *Hearts Insurgent*, because, as Hardy explained, the original choice was too close to the title of a previously published novel (Charles Reade's *A Simpleton*).[2] Hardy even asked for the serial to be re-titled *The Recalcitrants*, but his request came too late, after the heading *Hearts Insurgent* had been set in type.

The international publication certainly helped to swell Hardy's fame or notoriety. *Harper's New Monthly Magazine*, based in New York, reached a wide American public; and *Harper's Monthly Magazine* (without the *New* and with different volume-numbers in its otherwise identical European edition), issued in London under the aegis of Osgood, McIlvaine & Company, distributed the same text to British and continental readers.[3] The instalments were proficiently illustrated by W. Hatherell.

Harper's New Monthly Magazine had commissioned a novel which should be 'in every respect suitable for a family magazine', and Hardy had promised that 'it would be a tale that could not offend the most fastidious maiden'; but, as he worked on it, he felt obliged to warn the editor that it 'was carrying him into unexpected fields' and therefore asked to be allowed to cancel the agreement.[4] No cancellation occurred, but, in response to requests from the editor, Hardy agreed to bowdlerize the text, drastically reducing its sexual frankness. For example: in the serial version, Jude marries Arabella not because she has seduced him and claims to be pregnant but because she falsely declares that she has received a postal offer of marriage from a rival suitor. When, after their separation, he encounters her again, at Christminster, he does not spend the night with her. At Aldbrickham Jude and Sue live in separate houses; Sue never copulates with Jude; and instead of bearing two children she merely adopts another child in addition to 'Father Time'. The scene of Sue's eventual sexual submission to Phillotson was also omitted. As in subsequent versions, however, Arabella does attract Jude's attention by throwing a pig's penis at him.[5]

By means of careful work before and at the proof stage, Hardy restored the novel's originally-envisaged boldness and frankness for the first book edition.[6] This was the London edition published by Osgood, McIlvaine & Co. on 1 November 1895 in one volume at six shillings. (The American first edition, issued by Harper, New York, on 9 November, had many petty differences in house style – in publishing-house editorial conventions of spelling and punctuation – but no substantive authorial differences from the London volume.)

In 1903 a 'New Edition' was published in Great Britain by Macmillan. This contained numerous revisions by Hardy, and it is clear that, for all his indignation at the critical attacks that the 1895 edition had provoked, he was prepared to modify the novel in the light of those attacks. For instance, the references to the pig's penis were toned down so that the missile became less conspicuous and its exact nature rather less evident. In the 1895 version, the pizzle draws the reluctant yet fascinated attention of Jude and Arabella, as here:

> She, too, looked in another direction, and took the piece as though ignorant of what her hand was doing. She hung it temporarily on the rail of the bridge, and then, by a species of mutual curiosity, they both turned, and regarded it . . . . .
>
> They talked a little more and a little more, as they stood regarding the limp object dangling across the hand-rail of the bridge.

In the 1903 version, their attention is directed rather towards each other:

> But she, slily looking in another direction, swayed herself backwards and forwards on her hand as it clutched the rail of the bridge, till, moved by amatory curiosity, she turned her eyes critically upon him . . . . .
>
> They talked a little more and a little more, as they stood regarding each other and leaning against the hand-rail of the bridge.[7]

Arabella herself, who, in the manuscript, the serial and the 1895 book, was termed a 'substantial female human', became (in a change to dismay latter-day feminist readers) a 'substantial female animal'.[8] Jude's Greek New Testament, which in 1895 was inconsistently described as both closed and open on the same occasion, was now consistently left open. Numerous smaller changes were made.

In 1912 appeared the Macmillan 'New Wessex' edition, and for this Hardy made considerable further revisions. The brawl occasioned by

Phillotson's forced resignation was made somewhat more farcical, and some sexual details were made more explicit. For instance, when Sue and Jude are refused accommodation because a householder observes that Sue is pregnant, the 1903 edition said 'The householder scrutinized Sue a moment', whereas the 1912 edition says 'The householder scrutinized Sue's figure a moment' – a change which makes clear that her pregnancy is conspicuous. A sequence of other modifications made Sue rather more sympathetic. Whereas the 1903 text said at one point that Jude and Sue 'kissed each other', the 1912 version says that they 'kissed close and long'. Her consoling words, previously 'You did kiss me just now, you know; and I didn't dislike you to, very much, Jude', became 'You did kiss me just now, you know; and I didn't dislike you to, I own it, Jude'. Her declaration to him, 'I agree! I ought to have known that you would conquer . . . . .', became 'I agree! I do love you. I ought to have known that you would conquer . . . . .'[9]

Given that the 1912 edition represented Hardy's careful reappraisal of the material, it is understandable that this was the text which tended to be reprinted by subsequent British editors. In the United States, in contrast, the 1895 version dominated reprints until 1957, when the Harper's Modern Classics edition issued the text of 1912. By 1990, the editions published by Harper, Penguin Books, Macmillan, Oxford University Press and Norton all maintained the 'New Wessex' text. This editorial consensus did, however, have certain unfortunate consequences. It meant, for example, that readers were then consulting a text which differed quite significantly from the historically important edition of 1895. It was that first edition which had attracted widespread attention from the reviewers and which had provoked the furore that largely contributed to Hardy's decision to cease novel-writing. Thus, readers of the reprints of the 1912 text were not seeing precisely the version which had been so important in Hardy's development; and, crucially, the text was out of phase with that famous or notorious critical furore of the 1890s. To judge the fairness or otherwise of those critical comments, it is proper that readers should see the text that provoked them. Furthermore, though the revisions of 1903 and 1912 represent the fruits of Hardy's later reflections, there is no guarantee that that older Hardy (who, after all, was in his sixties and seventies at those times) was a wiser author than the younger man who had completed the 1895 version. Sometimes the revisions mitigate (and thereby make more conventional) certain bold features of characterization and situation which were appropriate to the general thematic radicalism of the novel. Even where the text is unchanged, criticisms of, say, the sanctity of marriage were bolder when uttered in the context of the 1890s than were identical criticisms made in the somewhat less inhibited context of 1912.

In the light of these considerations, it is the 1895 text published in London by Osgood, McIlvaine & Company that is used for quotation in this present critical study. The choice ensures that the quoted material corresponds to what the various early critics, at that crucial time in the 1890s, saw and appraised. There is no 'definitive' text. The first edition has various flaws, and the revisions published in 1903 and 1912 have, arguably, reduced the impact of the original.

When we look back over the history of the modifications of *Jude the Obscure*, we see that Hardy was prepared to adulterate his novel in order to secure the substantial payments from *Harper's New Monthly*; that this mode of censorship operated far more forcefully in the case of such a 'family magazine' than in the case of more specialized periodicals like the *New Review*, *Cosmopolis* or *Savoy*; and that he and Osgood, McIlvaine & Co. (and Harper's in the United States) showed considerable courage in releasing the relatively unexpurgated text of the first book edition. The critical furore aroused by the book proved lucrative: within three months of *Jude*'s appearance, an advertisement in the *Saturday Review* declared that the British print-run already totalled twenty thousand copies. (Joseph Conrad's 'best seller', *Chance*, would take two years to sell thirteen thousand British copies after its appearance in 1914.)[10] Throughout the remaining years of Hardy's life, *Jude the Obscure* was frequently reprinted in various editions, notably Macmillan's Collected Edition in the 'Three-and-Sixpenny Library of Books by Popular Authors'. After his death, the flow of reprints continued, paperbacks enabling them to reach a wider readership; and the expiry of his copyright in 1978 ensured a new burgeoning of hardback and paperback reprints; and these, as we have seen, generally promulgated the historically anachronistic text of 1912.

A century after the bowdlerizing serial of *Jude the Obscure*, the situation for British authors is in some respects worse. Far fewer magazines serialize novels of merit; and, instead of being under moral pressure to bowdlerize fiction, authors are now under commercial pressure to include sexually explicit episodes even when such episodes have little relevance to the narrative. As the era of seventeenth-century Puritanism gave way to the era of Restoration libertinism, so the restraints and repressions in the Victorian tradition have given way to the licence and decadence of the late twentieth century. Hardy needed iconoclastic courage to be sexually frank in the book of *Jude*; a hundred years later, sexual plenitude in fiction often implies a mercenary conformism.

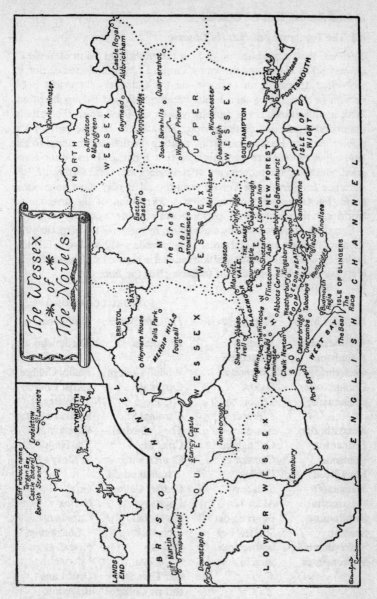

The Wessex map, authorized by Hardy and drawn by Stanford, which appeared in the first edition of *Jude the Obscure* (1895).

4.2 The Topography of *Jude the Obscure*

The map that is reprinted on p. 57 is the traditional 'Map of Wessex', authorized by Hardy and drawn by Stanford for the collected edition of 1895–7; it appeared, for example, on the endpaper of the first book version of *Jude*. Since then it has become hallowed by republication. With modifications, it has repeatedly been reprinted down the years in innumerable editions of the novels. Thus it has become part of the public image of Hardy, graphically relating the fictional material to the landscapes of southern and south-western England. It has done some good, clarifying the movements of characters and emphasizing the importance to Hardy of a known terrain; and it may have done some harm, by suggesting too immediate a correlation of the imaginative world with the geographical specificities of nineteenth-century England.

Certainly, Hardy was ready and willing, by means of the map, the 1911 'General Preface' and his memoirs, to help readers who wished to identify in the real world the various locations named in his works. Using such aids, it is easy enough to prepare the following lists for *Jude*:

(OXFORD LOCATIONS)

Fictional Name	Real Location	Fictional Name	Real Location
Aldbrickham	Reading	Beersheba	The Jericho district
Alfredston	Wantage		
Casterbridge	Dorchester	Biblioll College	Balliol College
Christminster	Oxford	Cardinal College	Christ Church College
Cresscombe	Letcombe Basset	Cardinal St.	St Aldate's St.
Kennetbridge	Newbury	The Cathedral	Christchurch
Leddenton	Gillingham	Chief St.	The High
Lumsdon	Cumnor	Church with Italian porch	St Mary's
Marygreen	Fawley		
Melchester	Salisbury	Crozier College	Oriel
Quartershot	Aldershot	Fourways	Carfax
Sandbourne	Bournemouth	Octagonal chamber	Cupola of Sheldonian
Shaston	Shaftesbury		
Stoke-Barehills	Basingstoke	Oldgate College	New College
Wintoncester	Winchester		
		Old Time St.	Oriel Lane
		Rubric College	Brazenose
		St Silas	St Barnabas
		Theatre of Wren	Sheldonian

While being ready to assist readers in relating the fictional places to real places, Hardy was understandably keen to emphasize the differences between fiction and fact. His description of locations, he declared, was 'done from the real – that is to say, has something real for its basis, however illusively treated . . . . . [N]o detail is guaranteed . . . . . the portraiture of fictitiously named towns and villages was only suggested by certain real places, and wantonly wanders from inventorial descriptions of them . . . . .'[11] Again, there is a typically guarded reference in the *Later Years*:

Lord Rosebery took occasion in a conversation to inquire 'why Hardy had called Oxford "Christminster".' Hardy assured him that he had not done anything of the sort, 'Christminster' being a city of learning that was certainly suggested by Oxford, but in its entirety existed nowhere else in the world but between the covers of the novel under discussion.[12]

Hardy's response is partly evasive. He was obviously right to say that while Christminster was 'suggested by Oxford', the fictional city through which Jude and Sue walk differs from the historical city in being an imaginative location with uniquely fictional data. On the other hand, Christminster is far more like Oxford than it is like, say, Cambridge: not only is its geographical location precisely correspondent with that of Oxford, as the 'Wessex' map emphasizes, but also the alumni recalled in detail by Jude and the narrator (Jonson, Ken, Addison, Gibbon, Wesley, Peel, Arnold, Browning, Swinburne) are specifically *Oxonienses*; and its Tractarian movement is specifically cited. Yet the changes made to various names, whether names of locations or of people, do introduce a very fruitful ambiguity into the reader's response. What happens is that the historical Oxford becomes a shimmering presence which moves into and out of imaginative focus. When it moves out of focus, it is displaced by our imaginative recognition of 'Christminster' as a *representative* locality – representative of wider forces in the cultural and social world. The disguises, though often transparent, become at such times relatively opaque as the general thematic significances of the narrative press upon us. The very name 'Christminster', after all, means etymologically 'monastery devoted to Christ', so it serves (as the name 'Oxford' could not) to remind us of both Jude's aspirations – the educational and the religious. It keeps the name of Christ before us, and thus emphasizes the hypocritical lack of charity and love which Jude finds in the supposedly Christian world; and it particularly emphasizes the cruel irony that the workman denied access to the University himself possesses various attributes of Christ, the carpenter's

59

son. The satiric animus of the name 'Sarcophagus College' speaks for itself.

Thus, as a realist and craftsman of literature, Hardy was right to declare that he had researched his locations; while, as an imaginative writer with the artist's ability to invest topographical facts with general significances (historical, cultural, political), he was also right to affirm his prerogative to transform them: the 'Preface' to *Jude* declares that the novel seeks 'to give shape and coherence to a series of seemings, or personal impressions'.[13] What is important but harder to specify is the complex process engendered in the reader by fiction which so often invites an identification of a fictional with a real locality while also offering a distinctive totality of vision unique to the creative imagination of the author himself.

The effects of the recurrent use of a 'Map of Wessex' in so many editions of Hardy's works have been very diverse. One effect has been to proclaim Hardy as 'The Author of Wessex' – to emphasize a co-ordinating territory of the fiction. The reader's attention is visually drawn to the ways in which, though his novels and tales may differ markedly from each other in many respects, there is a common grounding to them provided by an environment derived from nineteenth-century geographical realities. Repetition and overlapping of locations in successive works of fiction can have a cumulative imaginative effect; while reading one novel we may carry over into the imagination information derived from a previous novel with a similar or overlapping setting. Furthermore, as location is linked to location (and as characters sometimes recur) there may be generated the sense of a meta-fictional territory, one closely related to reality and from which all the completed works of fiction may be regarded as only a selection. ('Meta' means 'beyond'. Conrad and Kipling achieve a meta-fictional effect by their use of the same characters and places in different works.) The reader's imagination is prompted to extend the literary hinterland.

Repetition of the map may, however, make that territory seem too static. The Wessex of the novels is a region undergoing change and disruption. The map shows no railways, but repeatedly in the novels the railway is a crucial agent of change, affecting distant rural localities and binding the provinces more and more to an economy directed from London. The absence of London from the map may encourage some readers to think too much of 'rural Hardy' and to forget the ways in which the metropolis and urbanization impinge on the lives of the characters. In *Jude*, Sue has lived and worked in the city for two years before going to Christminster; Arabella worked in industrial

Aldbrickham before meeting Jude; and the metropolis has sent forth the architect who arranges the devastation of the ancient church at Marygreen. Jude and Sue inhabit a world of telegrams, rapid rail travel, *and* and the speedy dissemination of information and ideas by newspapers, *mail* books and magazines. The contrast with *Under the Greenwood Tree* makes evident that the story of Wessex unfolded in the main sequence of Hardy's works is a sombre story of the gradual erosion of the rural communities and their traditions by the subversive and disruptive forces of a modern urbanized civilization.

Another effect of that Wessex map, then, is to encourage the kind of reader who enjoys both mental and touristic nostalgia. Coach and train excursions may be made to 'Hardy country', and hotels and restaurants may exploit the literary connection. The tourist industry and the publishing trade thus aid and abet each other. Certainly, knowledge of *Jude* will make Oxford more interesting for a visitor; and a knowledge of Oxford will make *Jude* more interesting. On the other hand, cultural tourism may obscure the fact that the power of *Jude* lies in its texture: in its vivid embodiment of Hardy's determination to address problems of sexuality, class, inequality and moral hypocrisy which are confined to no narrow location. We come closer to Hardy's imaginative territory by reflecting on the literary verve of his indictments of social injustice than by walking the streets of Oxford, book in hand, seeking to touch the very stones of his Biblioll College. As the novel's first epigraph reminds us, 'The letter killeth, but the spirit giveth life'; and the 'Map of Wessex' may sometimes have deflected attention from the spirit to the letter, from the sensitively intelligent to the mundanely topographical. If, however, you think of obvious contrasts between the static terrain that the map presents and the mobile ideological battleground that the novel depicts, then the hallowed 'Map of Wessex' may become appropriately replete with irony. If the map suggests provinciality, the texture of the novel remains cosmopolitan.

4.3 The Plot and Its Implications

Of course the book is all contrasts – or was meant to be in its original conception. Alas, what a miserable accomplishment it is, when I compare it with what I meant to make it! – *e.g.* Sue and her heathen gods set against Jude's reading the Greek testament; Christminster academical, Christminster in the slums; Jude the saint, Jude the sinner; Sue the pagan, Sue the saint; marriage, no marriage; &c., &c.[14]

Thus Hardy explained his scheme to Edmund Gosse. The plot of *Jude* is free from melodramatic intrigue (there is no conventional villainy) and is indeed governed by intricately planned ironic and thematic contrasts. If we isolate the plotting from its texture, we may gain an impression of deliberate and even elegant symmetries. (Hardy called it 'a sort of quadrille', 'almost geometrically constructed'.)[15] Jude is seduced by Arabella and marries her disastrously; he loves Sue and lives with her, ultimately disastrously; and, in his drunken downfall, he marries Arabella again. Symmetrically, Sue marries Phillotson disastrously, having been introduced to him by Jude; she loves Jude and lives with him, ultimately disastrously; and, in her religiose downfall, she marries Phillotson again. Jude's aspirations as a scholar are checked by Arabella; become renewed and coupled with religious ambitions; and are checked by the combination of Sue's scepticism and embittering experience. Sue, revolting against Christianity, seeks to embrace 'Hellenism', but reverts to superstitious religious belief, her regression coinciding with Jude's achievement of scepticism. Meanwhile, Arabella, who has turned to religion, has her newly gained faith undermined by a return of desire for Jude. Phillotson's plan to enter the University and the Church prompts Jude's similar ambitions; and Phillotson's failure is repeated in accentuated form by Jude. Generally, the function of these symmetrical mismatches and related counterpoints in attitude is to accentuate the pervading sense of cruel irony.

Thus, when it is isolated in summary form, the plot of *Jude* may give the impression of elegant concentration and terseness. Considered in greater detail, the plot may appear to be the vehicle of a 'willed' pessimism: a pessimism imposed by the author so insistently as to defy plausibility at times – the literary vice of vicarious self-pity.[16] There is considerable evidence that Hardy's determination to make pessimistic and even satiric points has led to some contorted and contrived ordination of the novel's events. Although this has long been a critical orthodoxy, it is one which seems to be vindicated by numerous details of the plot-structure. Certainly, the author concedes, though with a parenthetical warning, that Jude and Sue did enjoy happiness for a while: 'That the twain were happy – between their times of sadness – was indubitable'; and we are told: 'That complete mutual understanding, in which every glance and movement was as effectual as speech for conveying intelligence between them, made them almost the two parts of a single whole.'[17] That phrase 'the two parts of a single whole' echoes the suggestion in Plato's *The Symposium* that love is 'the desire and pursuit of the whole' by two individuals who were once halves of a single living entity; and Saint-Pierre's Paul and Virginia, with whom Jude and Sue are compared, resemble 'the children of Leda, enclosed within the same shell'.[18] But Hardy's brief account of the harmonious phase in the life of Jude and Sue has the tactical purpose of offsetting his satiric observations on marriage. At this time, Sue and Jude are unmarried, and their harmony is contrasted with the discordancy which Hardy depicts as endemic in marriage.

Arabella, watching them at the agricultural show, remarks shrewdly: 'How she sticks to him! . . . . . I fancy that they are not married, or they wouldn't be so much to one another as that . . .' As for Arabella and her husband Cartlett, '[T]hey left the tent together, this pot-bellied man and florid woman, in the antipathetic, recriminatory mood of the average husband and wife of Christendom.'[19] This satiric scorn against marriage is maintained throughout the novel: in the first chapter we are reminded that 'many a man had made love-promises to a woman at whose voice he had trembled by the next seed-time after fulfilling them in the church adjoining'.[20] When Jude and Sue go to the Registrar's Office, the two couples who are getting married imply a dismal commentary on wedlock. The first comprises a soldier 'sullen and reluctant' and a bride 'sad and timid; she was soon, obviously, to become a mother, and she had a black eye'. The second couple is little better: the groom has just been released from jail, and is 'an ill-favoured man, closely cropped, with a broad-faced, pock-marked woman on his arm, ruddy with liquor and the satisfaction of being on the brink of a gratified desire'. As we have seen, the satire becomes most overt near the end of the novel, when the landlord, on seeing Arabella kiss Jude, doubts that they are married; but when he hears Arabella abuse Jude and fling a shoe at his head, 'he recognized the note of ordinary wedlock' and concludes that 'they must be respectable'. The phrasing is that of Hardy at his most drily mordant.[21]

The presence of satiric features does raise a problem. In satire, we know that the author exaggerates and distorts evils, vices and follies; we accept such exaggerations and distortions as part of the satiric convention, and ask not 'Is this accurate?' but 'Is this a vivid and entertaining exaggeration or distortion?' But, for much of the time, the prevailing convention of *Jude* is realism, not satire; by its endeavour to be faithful in detail to human conduct in particular locations at a particular historical time, the writer invites us to appreciate the accuracy of representation as we are surprised into recognition of the significance of the familiar. Thus, some tension exists between the accuracy of realism and the stylization of satire. Hardy's animus against marriage is so marked as to seem to be imposing itself on the plot. All the marriages depicted in detail are unhappy or acrimonious, while marriages glimpsed in the background seem sordid or ill-fated; and repeatedly the general rule is offered that the only happy couples are unmarried ones – and even then, their happiness is likely to be brief. Indeed, Jude and Sue seem doubly trapped. If they were to marry, Sue would feel constrained and oppressed; but by remaining unmarried, they incur ostracism and persecution.

Thus, one of the vectors of the plot is Hardy's evident desire to vent criticism of 'the famous contract – sacrament I mean'[22] of marriage. An even more important vector is his animus against the conception of divine providence. Here the poem 'Hap' (quoted in section 3.2) is particularly relevant. The novel may initially give the impression that Jude is a victim of mere bad luck ('Crass Casualty', as the poem terms it); but his bad luck is so great and so repeated as to give the impression that 'Crass Casualty' has some resemblance to a hostile God. The plot is so determinedly anti-providential as to offer support for an anti-theistic rather than an agnostic reading of its dominant metaphysic. Coincidences, for which Hardy's plots are notorious, here operate repeatedly to produce misery rather than happiness; and the effect of repetition is to make them seem more than mere chance – rather, the manipulation of victims by some victimizing 'President of the Immortals'. Suffering may thus become obfuscated (or 'mystified') as victimization.

Of the coincidences, major instances include these. In III.viii, we are told that Jude, at Melchester, arranges to meet Sue at Alfredston in order to visit their ailing Aunt Drusilla. Before the meeting, he goes to Christminster, where he has been offered a job, but then declines it. He enters a tavern for a drink, and, by wild coincidence, this is the very tavern where Arabella, who had previously been living in Australia, is now working. Consequently, he spends the night with Arabella (travelling by rail to Aldbrickham for the purpose) and misses his appointment with Sue. The meeting with Arabella is one bizarre coincidence; another soon follows. When Sue leaves Phillotson and elopes with Jude, they go to Aldbrickham; a youth chooses a hotel for them; and it is tardily discovered to be the very hotel (of all the hotels in the town) where Jude had spent the night with Arabella; furthermore, by chance, Sue finds that she has been allocated the very room where the two had slept on that previous occasion. Indeed, the frequency with which chance enables Arabella to encounter Jude is remarkable: at the agricultural fair, for instance, she and her husband have chosen to travel fifty miles from London and have reached the very place where, as it happens,

Jude and Sue are spending the day. Again, at the spring fair at Kennet-bridge, Arabella yet again coincidentally meets Jude. Given the mobility of the characters and the thousands of miles (including a voyage to Australia and back) spanned by their various journeys, the frequency of meeting defies probability. It is typical of the subordination of event to irony that even in the closing pages of the novel, when Jude is dying in Christminster, Arabella should be leeringly encountered by physician Vilbert, who, so many years previously, had helped her to ensnare Jude. In Hardy's works, the pleasures given to the reader by incisive irony may often compensate for the strain imposed by violated plausibility.

If such plotting implies a metaphysic, that metaphysic seems, in *Jude*, more antitheistic than agnostic. Yet the use of patent coincidences may sometimes give the impression less of a hostile supernatural power than of a wilfully pessimistic author, who, in his endeavour to indict the cruelty of the creation, runs the risk of alienating those readers who infer that if obvious manipulation of events is required to sustain the metaphysic, the metaphysic can command little belief. That wilfulness which strains credulity is apparent, notoriously, in the characterization of young Father Time, that dismal spokesman of doom, and in the scene of the 'slaughter of the innocents', the suicide of Time after his murder of two siblings. Another sign of willed pessimism is the sheer extent of the ironic symmetries. That Sue should return to the arms of Phillotson may, on its own, seem credible enough, but when that reversion is followed so closely by the reversion of Jude to Arabella, the symmetries may seem more neat than credible. One large paradox of the novel is that Hardy, who detested cruelty and therefore wished his readers to sympathize with the victims of cruelty, runs the risk of seeming cruel to his creations: we may sometimes feel that it is not a President of the Immortals but one Thomas Hardy who is sporting with his victims. As Swinburne wrote to Hardy, after reading *Jude*: 'But . . . . . how cruel you are! Only the great and awful father of "Pierrette" and "L'Enfant Maudit" [i.e., Balzac] was ever so merciless to his children.'[23]

Another peculiarity of the plotting is the marked acceleration in the last third of the novel. In the first third, the author has time for detailed exposition of scene and character; but gradually the pace accelerates, and towards the end there is a jerky rapidity of momentum. This seems partly to be a sign of failing patience, of a hastiness in completing the work. The fiercely, cogently and persuasively ironic structures of the earlier part of the plot give way to the more bitter, automatic and strained ironic structures that ensue. Partly, however, this may be a sign of Hardy's narrative experimentalism, for there is some anticipation of impressionistic techniques: impressionistic in the sense that the narrative unfolds as a series of vivid brief scenes, their connecting material being elided or compressed. When Hardy said that *Jude the Obscure* offered 'impressions', he not only emphasized the provisionality of the work but also invoked Impressionist art, in which the painter seeks to offer vivid glimpses of the variable rather than to 'tell a story' in Pre-Raphaelite style. And certainly, it could also be argued that Hardy is moving into the territory of expressionism.

Expressionist art (visual and literary) is characterized by the starkness with which it presents a distorted, often tormented, vision: the world depicted seems to be expressive of a grim, disturbed or disorientated state of mind. Expressionism flourished in the period 1870–1930; its famous exemplars were Vincent van Gogh, Edvard Munch, Emil Nolde, August Strindberg, Gottfried Benn and Franz Kafka; its great precursors were Shakespeare, in the most turbulent scenes of *King Lear*, and Georg Büchner in *Woyzeck*; and its rearguard includes Samuel Beckett and Harold Pinter. The world of *Woyzeck*, for instance, seems harsh, grim, nightmarish; characters seem grotesque, deranged, or depressively fatalistic; Woyzeck himself, partly crazed, partly pathetic victim and partly seer of cosmic cruelty, is swept along into jealousy and murder; violent irrationality seems endemic in the universe.

Nowadays, a reader's memories of expressionism may thus influence judgement of *Jude the Obscure*. If, by realistic standards, Hardy's coincidental plotting and related insistent pessimism seem flaws, a critic may be tempted to offer the defence that realistic criteria are inappropriate: we should rather see that Hardy is offering an expressionistic vision, to be judged less by its plausibility and more by its intensity. What one reader condemns as implausible contrivance another may defend as consistent stylization. The main objection to this defence is that whereas the worlds of *Woyzeck* or of Kafka's *The Castle* are, from the outset, depicted as expressionistically stylized, so that we rapidly sense the departure from customary realism, in Hardy's novel the realism is dominant from the outset, and consequently, though his techniques do veer somewhat (particularly towards the end) in the direction of the impressionistic, of the symbolic (Father Time) and of the expressionistic (in the insistence on life's harshness), the firmness with which the historically contemporaneous has been established means that these veerings are likely to be sensed as strains, tensions or inconsistencies.

Critics often assume that the appropriate criteria for responding to a literary work are those which maximize the intelligibility of that work. In the case of *Jude*, such criteria are those of a realism qualified by strong ironic and thematic co-ordination; and, though there are modulations towards the expressionistic, the symbolic and the impressionistic, we lose more intelligibility than we gain if we seek to make the expressionistic criterion the dominant, for then we have to ignore that detailed historic specificity of reference. The worlds depicted in *The Castle* and *Waiting for Godot* are timeless limbos; the world of *Jude the Obscure* is distinctly that of southern England in the period 1880–95, with its railways, telegraphy, cultural debates, social divisions. There is, however, some continuity between these works. *Jude the Obscure* is a pilgrim's progress of a pilgrim doomed to frustration, as is *The Castle*. Furthermore, in *The Castle* and *Waiting for Godot*, as in *Jude the Obscure*, the metaphysic is ambiguous, veering between the atheistic and the antitheistic: between the sense that God is absent and the sense that God is present, observant and hostile.

One notable critic of *Jude the Obscure*, Irving Howe, has asserted: 'Not by its fullness or probability as a rendering of common life, but by its power and coherence as a vision of modern deracination – so must the book be judged.'[24] We can now readily understand why he said this. Thinking that *Jude* must be judged *either* as realism *or* as something else, and knowing that the plotting sometimes strains the sense of realism, Howe tries to vindicate the book by saying that we must opt for 'something else': and he suggests that it is an 'expressionist' work which expresses 'a vision of modern deracination'. Howe, like other critics, is perhaps too fond of thinking in terms of 'either/or'. The plot of *Jude the Obscure* offers a realism which is strongly inflected, modified, and at times contorted and distorted, by the demands of irony directed against religious providentialism, 'holy wedlock' and other social institutions, class injustice and moral hypocrisy. That irony sometimes impels the writing towards satire and black comedy. The vigour and incisiveness of the plotting derive largely from the same moral indignation which, pressing to excess, leads at times to implausible contrivance. Within Hardy's moral imagination, as we have seen, there are tensions and contradictions which are reflected in some of the more awkward shifts from the relatively empirical to the relatively stylized in the work's structure. Since these tensions and contradictions are so ideologically and historically revealing, however, there is a sense in which even the novel's literary faults (which are clearly outweighed by its superb merits) add to its cultural interest.

Joseph Conrad once remarked that, over many years, he had become so affectionately familiar with Dickens's *Bleak House* that 'its very weaknesses are more precious to me than the strength of other men's work'.[25] I feel the same about *Jude the Obscure*. Given that it appeared in 1895, Hardy's novel displays such moral and political courage, voiced with so much indignant verve, that even when the verve declines to an impatient assertiveness it may be hard for the reader not to understand and forgive the author. Thus, critical judgements of this novel may often be impure: literary criteria will often be infiltrated by criteria of the kind we might use when judging a friend who, though sometimes bitter and cantankerous, is on the whole courageously humane. The reactionary critical doctrine of 'the Death of the Author' (advocated by a long-deceased author, Roland Barthes)[26] overlooked the fact that the personality implicit in the writings of a major novelist is as unique as one's thumbprint; so judgements of the implied personality inevitably, and properly, are inseparable from judgements of the literary merit. That implied personality, implicit in the texture of the works, differs from the personality which the author would present if interviewed in the flesh. Nevertheless, no work makes adequate sense if divorced from its historical context, and the author is an essential part of that context.

4.4 Thematic Tensions

Plot-summaries are normally diachronic: they tell us how event leads to event in course of time. Theme-summaries are normally synchronic: they specify thematic topics which provide co-ordinators of elements of plot, characterization and description; and the topics may remain constant, though their local manifestation may be variable. Themes tend to be pliable and capacious. For example, there are few novels which cannot be said to contain themes summarizable as 'the transition from innocence to experience', 'the quest for fulfilment' or 'the conflict of reality and illusion'. All three are present in *Jude the Obscure*. The reader will notice one obvious rule: the briefer the thematic summary, the more obvious or platitudinous it will seem; the longer the thematic summary, the more interesting but more disputable it may become. It is a sign of the jagged, fiercely engaged, ideologically turbulent nature of *Jude the Obscure* that any detailed scansion of its themes soon reveals tensions or contradictions. The following selection illustrates this point.

4.4.1 RELIGIOUS THEMES

As we have noted, the metaphysic of this novel has tensions which move towards contradiction. The text suggests variously that God is absent; that a creative Will may be existent but not yet evolved from unawareness to awareness of the sorry plight of the creation; and that God is existent but punitive. Although the last of these possibilities is defined, at the time of Sue's relapse, as an illusion generated by misfortune, numerous features of the text (including the repeated allusions to the Book of Job, and particularly the very full citation of Job by the dying Jude) intermittently evoke the notion of supernaturally ordained suffering. Jude is, in one obvious respect, a more unfortunate victim than Job; for, whereas the latter was eventually recompensed richly for his woes ('So the LORD blessed the latter end of Job more than his beginning'),[27] Jude dies in solitary poverty.

A related theme concerns the validity and value of organized religion, of the Church as a social institution. The old parish church at Marygreen is described as 'the ancient temple to the Christian divinities'.[28] The phrasing is significantly sceptical: 'temple' suggests that it may be little different from a place of pagan worship; 'Christian divinities' astutely implies that though Christianity is supposedly monotheistic, the diversification of God as several entities (God the Father, God the Son and God the Holy Ghost), not to mention the roles of Mary and the other saints, has given Christianity a resemblance to polytheistic paganism. Sue describes the saints as 'the demi-gods in [Jude's] Pantheon';[29] and she claims that her statuettes of Venus and Apollo are those of St Mary and St Peter. By suggesting points of continuity between Christian and pre-Christian religion, Hardy questions Christianity's claim to uniqueness. (Sir James Frazer's *The Golden Bough*, which emphasized the continuity between fertility-cults, pagan religion and Christianity, had begun to appear in 1890.)[30] Jude's studies of religion are seen to be heroic in their dedicated labour, yet also anachronistic; the Church Fathers offer little sustenance in the modern world in which, according to Sue, the railway-stations have superseded the cathedrals. Repeatedly, religious ideals and precepts are criticized or mocked by mundane actualities. Sue's workplace and hostel at Christminster and her training college at Melchester are seen as joyless, repressive, puritanical establishments. Jude is filled with religious exaltation by a hymn he hears, and seeks out the composer: to his disillusionment, the composer grumbles that there's no money to be made from hymns, and offers him a wine list.

The first epigraph of the novel is taken from 2 Corinthians III: 6: 'The letter killeth, but the spirit giveth life.' In the Victorian England through which Jude and Sue move, the letter of the church's moral code ('Thou shalt not commit adultery') is respected and often punitively enforced; the spirit, the spirit of Christ who championed the meek and lowly (and the woman taken in adultery), is everywhere denied. Typically, Jude and Sue are dismissed from their work of repainting the Ten Commandments because they are thought to be unmarried; and, for the same reason, Jude is obliged to resign from the committee of the 'Artizans' Mutual Improvement Society'. Phillotson, who shows charity to Sue when she wishes to leave him, is forced to leave his post at his school.

The novel's very title, *Jude the Obscure*, is variously ominous. The 'General Epistle of Jude' (in the New Testament) is itself 'obscure', in the sense that it is short, easily overlooked, and rather mysterious, for it was written to some unknown community in the primitive church; only after considerable hesitation by the Bible's compilers was its status agreed to be canonical rather than apocryphal. St Jude's epistle offers warnings against those Christians who allow themselves to be corrupted by fleshly lusts: 'these *filthy* dreamers defile the flesh, despise dominion, and speak evil of dignities' – a verse which adds resonance to one of the original titles of Part I of Hardy's novel, 'The Dreamer', and to Jude's seduction by Arabella. Perhaps it was Hardy's sense of social injustice that led him to underline in the epistle a verse which denounces those who command admiration 'because of advantage'.[31] St Jude (a martyr clubbed to death) is the patron saint of lost or hopeless causes, therefore being ironically appropriate to his namesake who, quixotically, strives in vain to realize his ideals in an inimical world.

Sometimes, in addition, Hardy's Jude is briefly and with varying degrees of irony linked to Jesus, as when the young lad hubristically declares, 'I'll be her beloved son, in whom she shall be well pleased' (echoing Matthew III: 17), or when Jude plans to begin his ministry at the age of thirty, like 'his exemplar when he first began to teach in Galilee', or when he sits down 'by the well, thinking as he did so what a poor Christ he made' (alluding to John IV: 6, where Christ 'sits on a well' during the journey to commence his ministry). Sue remarks that leaving Kennetbridge for Christminster is 'like coming from Caiaphas to Pilate'.[32] By means of such references and the general depiction of Jude's frustrated idealism, his persecution, his suffering and early death, Hardy intermittently invites us to think of Jude as partly analogous to a modern Christ. He is no 'Christ-symbol', for these analogies are only intermittent and are tinged with irony.

In *Jude the Obscure*, one technique which gathers thematic force is that of discordance and parody. There are repeatedly 'rude awakenings' for Jude as his aspirations clash with discordant realities; whether he is being punished by Farmer Troutham, assailed by a pig's pizzle or dismissed by the Master of Biblioll College, he experiences the 'satires of circumstance'. Hardy deploys a related variety of demeaning parodies. The killing of the pig by Jude and Arabella resembles in various details a burlesque of the killing of Duncan by Macbeth and Lady Macbeth; Arabella, when seducing Jude, is a parody-Delilah; and Jude, reciting the creed to the crowd in a pub, parodies a prophet among his disciples. Jerusalem is demeaningly represented in the inaccurate cardboard model; Christminster is ludicrously transformed into 'Christminster cakes' made of gingerbread.

4.4.2 'GINS AND SPRINGES'

The text is interlaced by imagery of gins, springes and snares. A 'gin' (engine for entrapment) was a powerful spring-trap fitted with metal teeth. A 'springe' was a snare with noose and spring. By means of such imagery Hardy seeks to co-ordinate the various kinds of entrapment, sexual, social and even metaphysical, which beset Jude and Sue. The imagery may have been suggested by the Book of Job (XVIII: 8–10), which says of the sinner:

> For he is cast into a net by his own feet, and he walketh upon a snare.
>
> The gin shall take *him* by the heel, *and* the robber shall prevail against him.
>
> The snare is laid for him in the ground, and a trap for him in the way.

When Jude realizes that he has been tricked into marriage to Arabella, we are told: 'He was inclined to inquire what he had done, or she lost, for that matter, that he deserved to be caught in a gin which would cripple him, if not her also, for the rest of a life-time?'[33] The imagery becomes tangibly manifest when, at Shaston, Jude hears the cry of a rabbit tortured in a gin; he kills the creature to release it from its agony; and thus he encounters Sue, who has similarly been awakened by the cry, and who tells him of her entrapment in marriage to Phillotson. Later, he reflects thus:

Strange that his first aspiration – towards academical proficiency – had been checked by a woman, and that his second aspiration – towards apostleship – had also been checked by a woman. 'Is it,' he said, 'that the women are to blame; or is it the artificial system of things, under which the normal sex-impulses are turned into devilish domestic gins and springes to noose and hold back those who want to progress?'[34]

Trap within trap within trap. Jude, for all his aspirations, is ensnared by the sexual demands of his body: he is victim of 'constant internal warfare between flesh and spirit'.[35] Hence the epigraph to Part V of the book, the passage from Marcus Antoninus warning that man's 'aërial' and 'fiery' parts are 'overpowered here in the compound mass the body'. Jude finds himself ensnared by marriage to an unsuitable partner, the institution of marriage being part of 'the artificial system of things'. In marriage, and more markedly in his cohabitation with Sue, he seems trapped by the hereditary or genetic doom besetting sexual partnerships of the Fawleys. Like other humans, Jude is also trapped as a sensitive being within a world which affords an inappropriately harsh environment. As Phillotson puts it, 'Cruelty is the law pervading all nature and society; and we can't get out of it if we would!'[36] The imagery of snares finally has antitheistic metaphysical implications, to the extent that Jude may seem to have been ensnared by a hostile supernatural force.

There is a clear tension, moving towards contradiction, in Hardy's view of the sexual instincts. Part of the time his view seems 'permissive': here the novel says, in effect, 'If people wish to live together and copulate outside wedlock, let them do so; marriage often binds partners cruelly.' Phillotson even remarks, 'I don't see why the woman and the children should not be the unit without the man'; and Sue later echoes that matriarchal notion:

'I *may* hold the opinion that, in a proper state of society, the father of a woman's child will be as much a private matter of hers as the cut of her under-linen, on whom nobody will have any right to conjecture.'[37]

The novel also suggests that true joy may be found in the unconstrained sexuality of unmarried partners. As Sue puts it:

'We said ..... that we would make a virtue of joy. I said it was Nature's intention, Nature's law and *raison d'être* that we should be joyful in what instincts she afforded us – instincts which civilization had taken upon itself to thwart.'[38]

On the one hand, then, the novel advocates the joy to be found in sexual freedom; yet, on the other hand, the novel suggests that aspiring individuals may repeatedly be betrayed and ensnared by the demeaning demands of the flesh. It is a tension between Hardy the liberal, advocating (as Blake, Shelley and J. S. Mill had done) a more tolerant and less repressive society, and Hardy the evolutionary pessimist, who feels (as Schopenhauer had felt) that humans are unfortunate hybrids, insufficiently evolved from the primitive bestial heritage. Schopenhauer, we have noted, remarked: 'If the act of procreation were . . . . . a matter to be decided on the basis of purely rational considerations, is it likely the human race would still exist?'[39]

A minor variant on the theme of 'snares, gins and springes' is the 'Samson and Delilah' theme. When Arabella first takes Jude to an inn, a picture of Samson and Delilah hangs ominously on the wall; when the marriage fails, Jude revisits the tavern and notes the same picture; and when Arabella eventually recaptures the demoralized Jude, he is described as 'her shorn Samson'.[40] An august biblical precedent is thus cited for Jude's entrapment and degradation.

In contrast, it may be noted that the persistent emphasis on formal marriage as a trap is partly challenged by the novel's concession that divorce is readily obtainable, and, indeed, is more easily obtainable by the lowly and obscure than by the high and mighty. Similarly, its stress on the penalization of couples who seek to live together outside wedlock is somewhat weakened by the fact that Sue crucially brings about disaster by eventually declaring, instead of maintaining the concealment of, her unmarried state. In the former case, the modern facilitation of divorce is evidence of that social progress towards greater individual liberty which the imagery of 'gins and springes' often seems to deny. In fact, that imagery of ensnarement may have both conservative and anti-conservative consequences. To the extent that the imagery suggests a perennial and inexorable situation, it seems conservative; to the extent that it evokes indignation leading to reforms (to reduce the resemblance between marriage and a trap, for instance), it may be progressive.

Hardy argued that he was actually a meliorist (a person believing in the possibility of progress towards better conditions), albeit in the sense defined in his poem 'In Tenebris': 'If way to the Better there be, it exacts a full look at the Worst.'[41] Nevertheless, in *Jude*, relatively heavy emphasis is placed on 'the Worst', while relatively little is said about any 'way to the Better'. It could be argued that Hardy has obfuscated matters by mingling social evils which could be rectified with large-scale evils about which little can be done: both small matters (amenable to legislation) and large matters (like the evolutionary struggle, or the anomaly of human awareness in an impersonal universe) are bonded by that imagery of gins and springes. A related factor is that though Jude and Sue are so alert to a variety of liberal ideas current in their time, they seem to have no awareness of the turbulent and much-publicized emergence of socialist and trade-unionist ideas in their period; so their isolation is heightened by conspicuous omissions from the novel's field of social reference. The omissions are partly explained by the distrust of radicalism noted by Hardy in his journal for 1888:

I find that my politics really are neither Tory nor Radical. I may be called an Intrinsicalist. I am against privilege derived from accident of any kind, and am therefore equally opposed to aristocratic privilege and democratic privilege. (By the latter I mean the arrogant assumption that the only labour is hand-labour – a worse arrogance than that of the aristocrat, – the taxing of the worthy to help those masses of the population who will not help themselves when they might, etc.) Opportunity should be equal for all, but those who will not avail themselves of it should be cared for merely – not be a burden to, nor the rulers over, those who do avail themselves thereof.[42]

When Jude is dying, he says:

'I hear that soon there is going to be a better chance for such helpless students as I was. There are schemes afoot for making the University less exclusive, and extending its influence. I don't know much about it. And it is too late, too late for me!'[43]

What Jude has heard about is the campaign which resulted in the foundation in 1899 of Ruskin College, Oxford: the college, still very active today, which enables formally-unqualified working people to gain access to the university system. In his 'Postscript' to the novel, Hardy reported that some readers thought 'that when Ruskin College was subsequently founded it should have been called the College of Jude the Obscure'.[44] The sufferings and humiliations of Jude may have helped numerous working-class aspirants to elude the 'gins and springes' of economic disadvantage.

4.5 Aspects of Characterization

Cleanth Brooks once remarked that, in *The Waste Land*, T. S. Eliot 'works in terms of surface parallelisms which in reality make ironical contrasts, and in terms of surface contrasts which in reality constitute parallelisms'.[45] A similar principle can be seen in a very different area: the main characterizations of *Jude the Obscure*.

4.5.1 SUE

In broad outline, the characterization of Sue is clear and apparently unproblematic. Here is an intelligent, lively, attractive, intellectually emancipated young woman who marries unhappily and who, after living with her lover for a while, is so shocked by the deaths of their children that her theoretical emancipation is utterly undermined by religious guilt, with the result that, as a form of bitter penance, she returns self-sacrificially to her former husband. In this view, she can be seen as a tragic victim: a person of great potential whose vitality and independence are eventually destroyed by the partly internalized and partly external force of religion, a force aided and abetted by a society which is largely hostile to her kind of emancipation.

On a closer view, her character is remarkably problematic in its ambiguity; and the centre of ambiguity is what Jude terms her 'epicene nature'. In what sense is she epicene? In her combination of sexual allure and sexual inhibition, to what extent is she culpable? Is she a heartless flirt or a victim of predatory male sexuality? Is she a manipulative connoisseur of emotions or a person striving to maintain her integrity? Is she mercurially lively or infuriatingly inconstant? The questions multiply; but the narrative explicitly and implicitly defines her character as centrally unstable, enigmatic, ambiguous, and perplexing: she has 'colossal inconsistency'. Within the text, she provokes justifiably sympathetic and justifiably antipathetic responses. Sue is, in fact, the fullest and most complex development of a type of heroine who had fascinated Hardy from the first: the physically attractive, vivacious, intelligent and independent-minded young woman who readily attracts quite contrasting males, and who, consequently, becomes embarrassingly and sometimes tragically entangled with avid suitors. Even the earliest heroines (Cytherea, Fancy, Elfride) are clear precursors.

The case *against* Sue can readily be seen. At London, she lived with a student who was her first lover; but, though she defied convention in sharing accommodation with him, she insisted on preserving her virginity; and his early death is linked partly to his resultant anguish of frustration. On meeting Jude, she is eager to be his mentor and emancipator, chiding his religious conventionality; she tantalizes him by behaviour which oscillates between tender encouragement and temporary withdrawal. She marries Phillotson, who has been understandably encouraged and prompted by her smiling co-operation; yet before doing so, she insists on leading Jude to the altar in a rehearsal which for him is mortifying, even though for her it permits a subtle emotional gratification. The marriage to Phillotson founders because of her sexual denial, which reaches neurotic extremes when she first hides in a cupboard and later leaps from a window. Released by Phillotson (and unaware that his kindness to her wrecks his career), she hastens to her new life with Jude, but then dismays Jude by her initial determination not to sleep with him; and her resolve ends only when Arabella appears, so that, to defeat a rival, Sue acquiesces sexually. Yet she declines to marry Jude, largely because she fears that marriage would destroy spontaneity and deprive her of the right to deny him sexual intercourse when she chooses. The children die, partly because she has failed to offer Jude's son reasonable reassurance and has reinforced his gloom by her replies; and she provides opportunity for the infanticide by culpably leaving the children alone while she breakfasts with Jude in a different house. She knows that her return to Phillotson will utterly demoralize Jude, yet she not only returns but swears on the Bible never to see her lover again. So, at different times, she has inflicted frustration and misery on the anonymous student, on Phillotson and on Jude.

Certainly, she receives many telling rebukes. These come from Jude on many occasions, for her tendency to blow hot and cold, for the apparently wilful flirtatiousness, and for being 'so awfully merciless'; from Drusilla, for marrying a man 'that no woman of any niceness can stomach'; from Phillotson, for denying him and loving Jude. Sometimes the narrator notes critically her wilfulness as an exploitative 'epicure in emotions'.

On the other hand, one factor in mitigation is that Sue, in turn, can criticize and even condemn herself quite forthrightly; she experiences genuine (if temporary) remorse for much of the anguish she causes. More important is the sense that she is largely at the mercy of her own divided nature: the 'theoretic unconventionality' wars against the conventional within her; the flirtatiousness and emotional experimentalism is only partly under the governance of her will. (If Jude is divided between idealism and sexual desire, Sue is divided between independence and conventionality.) Perhaps most important of all is the ambiguity of her reluctance to submit to sexual intercourse with any of her diverse partners. This can at times appear an almost parodic version of the prudish Victorian notion that intercourse is a pleasure for a man but a painful duty for a virtuous woman. Yet what is more insistently suggested is that Sue is, in large part, simply more highly evolved than the men she encounters; and Hardy entertains the idea that, since sexual desire links us to the bestial, a highly evolved individual will seek 'Platonic love' rather than carnal love. As Sue puts it:

'Their [conventional] philosophy only recognizes relations based on animal desire. The wide field of strong attachment where desire plays, at least, only a secondary part, is ignored by them – the part of – who is it? – Venus Urania.'[46]

The problem of Sue's nature can be resolved, then, in two interlinked ways. One is to say that she is depicted by Hardy as a cultural palimpsest or unstable amalgam. At a time of ideological transition, she is trapped by the old ideologies of restraint, of religious guilt, even though she has sought to move on to a world of freer and relatively independent conduct; the conflict between the two eventually crushes her; her spirit is cowed by conventional pressures. The second way is to say that she expresses a profound division in Hardy himself where sexuality is concerned. On the one hand, he can see it as healthily natural, and can see social prudery and the institution of marriage as often curbing and fettering sexual joy; yet, on the other hand, he can distrust it as an aspect of 'Nature, red in tooth and claw'; as one of the snares of the spirit; as the source of new, potentially blighted lives. So the narrator lets us veer to and fro in evaluation of Sue's inhibition, while she herself struggles for a compromise between denial and acquiescence. She repeatedly expresses annoyance that marriage is 'a licence to be loved on the premises'; and Hardy, in a letter to Gosse, explained the implications:

[H]er sexual instinct [is] healthy as far as it goes, but unusually weak and fastidious . . . . ., and one of her reasons for fearing the marriage ceremony is that she fears it would be breaking faith with Jude to withhold herself at pleasure, or altogether, after it; though while uncontracted she feels at liberty to yield herself as seldom as she chooses. This has tended to keep his passion as hot at the end as at the beginning, and helps to break his heart. He has never really possessed her as freely as he desired.[47]

An instinct 'weak' yet 'fastidious': so she can be regarded both as lacking normal sexual vitality and as possessing an advanced sensitivity, just as she can be seen both as 'heartbreaking' in her restraint and as admirable in seeking to guard her integrity by eluding sexual constraint. What results is a fine study of character as a battleground of conflicting forces.

Her characterization is designed to imply the 'unpredicable' or 'unstateable',[48] but is given sharp memorability by a host of fine specific details. These include Aunt Drusilla's cameos of her tomboyish and precocious childhood (the pond-wading, the ice-skating with the boys, the recitation of 'The Raven' when 'she would knit her little brows and glare round tragically' at the empty air); then there is her intermittent preference for speaking obliquely, from behind some barrier or defence, whether it be a window-sill, a quotation, or the distance lent by written messages. Above all, her temperament and physical presence are rendered by numerous convincing particulars, ranging from her 'nervous motion', her quick affectionate spontaneity, her 'apple-like' breasts and 'liquid, untranslatable eyes', to her very handshake, in which her hand merely 'flits' through the other's.

A curious postscript to the characterization is provided by the manuscript of *Jude the Obscure*, in which a cancelled passage says that Jude at a tavern was overlooked by a picture of Susannah and the Elders. Sue's name was, therefore, associated with (and possibly derived from) the famous Susannah of the Apocrypha. There we are told that this beautiful woman aroused lust in two elders, who, initially rivals, combined forces to threaten her with death unless she submitted to their desires. She chose death; but the devout Daniel cross-examined the elders who falsely testified against her, their plot was exposed, and they were slain while she was freed. So, for Hardy, Sue's name not only meant, in Hebrew, 'lily' (connoting the pure, delicate and virginal); it also evoked the legend of a woman whose attractiveness led to her persecution by lustful males. No Daniel, alas, comes to the rescue of Susannah Bridehead.

4.5.2 JUDE

Examination questions about Hardy's later protagonists are commonly variants of the following: '"Not a truly tragic figure, but rather a hapless victim of cruel fate": Discuss with reference to Jude (or Tess).' Oscar Mandel, in his *A Definition of Tragedy*, offers a clear endorsement of the quoted view. For him, 'all tragedy concerns the will'; therefore 'we eliminate from our category the serious work of art which concerns itself with a victim':

The most famous of [Hardy's] perfect victims is Tess . . . . . Jude the Obscure is no luckier: that lugubrious manikin, or Schopenhauerian imp, little Father Time, decides to slaughter himself and Jude's children with him; whereupon Sue loses her faith and becomes a Christian, returns to her former husband, and leaves Jude to die a victim of alien forces he understands but cannot master. Hardy's philosophy (if we can flatter him with the term) makes tragedy all but impossible.[49]

Very tidy, if a little unkind. Tragedy, we are told, demands the striving will of the protagonist; a mere 'victim of alien forces' cannot be a tragic hero; therefore Jude is no tragic hero, and *Jude the Obscure* is not a tragedy.

It must be admitted that Hardy solicited such attentions. First, as we have seen, both the text of the novel and its preface invoked comparisons with great tragedies; and the 'General Preface' of 1912 cited 'our magnificent heritage from the Greeks'. Secondly, as is notorious, his ruthlessly ironic plotting can suggest the presence of a cruel destinal force (the 'malignant stars', in the narrator's phrase) which traps the unfortunate victim. Even if we were to accept Mandel's distinction, however, its application to *Jude the Obscure* would be challengeable. Hardy claimed that the novel depicted 'a deadly war waged between flesh and spirit' and 'the tragedy of unfulfilled aims'. Jude has his ambitions (to enter University and the Church) which are frustrated partly by his own nature – his sexual desires and emotional needs – and partly by social circumstances. Arguably, he is as much a striving and divided self as was many a celebrated tragic protagonist of the past; there is both inner and outer strife, and no simple acquiescence, at least until his final drunken submission to Arabella – and even then he rebelliously and almost suicidally seeks out Sue.

Mandel's definition of tragedy stipulates the central importance of a striving individual who commands our good will, and whose strivings lead ironically to his downfall.[50] Arguably, Jude fulfils these conditions. One obvious objection to this definition, however, is that while some great tragedies may seem to be focused on an individual, many concern the fortunes of a pair, or a group, or a dynasty, or a whole society. By concentrating on qualities of a single figure, Mandel underestimates the broad context within which that figure (or a group of figures) moves, and the effect is to reduce or elide the social and political dimensions of tragedy. In any case, there is an antiquated quality to the whole endeavour to construct a rigid definition and to award the prestigious accolade of 'tragedy' to works that fall within that definition, while consigning to an inglorious vestibule any works which fail to qualify. Some critics have resembled literary policemen seeking to keep trespassers away from a glamorous citadel. The term 'tragedy' is obviously used in many ways, some relatively rigorous and some quite loose and mild.

Followers of Ludwig Wittgenstein have usefully adopted his notion of definition based on 'family resemblances'. Morris Weitz, for example, has suggested that works in the tragic tradition are linked by a number of characteristics found with varying frequency.[51] Given some undisputed examples of literary tragedy, other works may be seen to have various features which relate them to those undisputed examples, and debate may ensue about the number of such features necessary to identify a work as a member of that family rather than of a different one. Within that family, two works may have no features in common; yet they may both belong to it because they each have features linking them to other exemplars. Flexibility increases further when we recognize that the tragic tradition is incessantly being reconstituted retrospectively; it is a critical construct reflecting the interests of the critic's age; and it tends to engorge even works which once might have been intended as anti-tragic, because those works still have an identity shaped by the antecedents, just as a rebellious son may have a nature shaped in part by his father. In short, the Platonic sense that there is some pure essence of tragedy to be captured by a lasting definition has been eroded by the modern empirical sense that the definition, nature, content and value of the tragic tradition are all matters of negotiation to establish a practical consensus: a consensus repeatedly evolving, breaking and re-forming as historical pressures change.

Hardy himself recognized this in *Jude*. If Hardy's anti-providentialism makes Jude a failed Dick Whittington, a Job without final compensation, a lesser Christ without disciples and without a resurrection, Hardy's scepticism tries to impel him towards a bleak world which, by some conventional standards, is 'post-tragic'. Within the text, tragic precedents are evoked (the House of Atreus, the Aeschylean sense of inherited doom), but when Jude dies alone, reciting Job, the Chorus is not the traditional tragic Chorus lamenting the death and meditating its moral significance; instead, it is the ironically contrapuntal Chorus of 'Hurrah! ..... Hurrah! ..... Hurrah!' from the undergraduates and spectators enjoying the 'Remembrance games'. Jude dies unremembered by them, a bitter outsider, a broken Quixote. As Sue had told him:

'You are Joseph the dreamer of dreams, dear Jude. And a tragic Don Quixote. And sometimes you are St. Stephen, who, while they were stoning him, could see Heaven opened. O my poor friend and comrade, you'll suffer yet!'[52]

His idealistic striving is defeated by a recalcitrant mundanity which includes the unjust class-system; and even tragic dignity of a conventional kind is eventually denied him by a world impervious to and unaffected by his ordeals. If Jude is, finally, a defeated victim, that does not necessarily make him a candidate who failed to qualify as tragic hero; it might make him a companion of Ibsen's Hedda Gabler, Chekhov's Ivanov, Conrad's Decoud, Miller's Loman and all those subsequent protagonists whose falls are denied traditional tragic resonance by the ironic ordinariness of the modern secular world. In that jarring, incongruous death-scene, Jude steps at last from the mesh cast over events by a moribund metaphysic; dying ignored, he can at least be resurrected as a modernist hero by the Chorus of Elders of Criticism.

Jude the Obscure can be seen as part of a project, sustained by various writers in the nineteenth and twentieth centuries, to incorporate in prose fiction some equivalences to tragedies designed for the theatre. It is also part of the long-term project to democratize tragedy by investing a middle-class or working-class figure with the representative significance accorded previously to kings, queens, princes or generals. The philosophical turbulence of *Jude the Obscure* expresses the painful transition from a theologically based world-view to a secular one. It reminds us that the tragic tradition has repeatedly been extended by *adversarial* literary works which both address and assail the assumptions of their august predecessors.

An individual's ancestry can soon be traced back to numerous families. If *Jude the Obscure* is a rebellious child within the tragic family, it can also be related to several other literary families. One is the *Bildungsroman*: the novel of the education of a hero who proceeds from infancy to maturity, learning salutary lessons about the world. The detailed attention given to Jude's self-education and its large implications places him firmly in the tradition of the *Bildungsroman*'s heroes. Another is the family of fictionalized autobiography, in which the protagonist's career has strong resemblances to, but critical differences from, that of the author; famous examples include *Jane Eyre* and *A Portrait of the Artist as a Young Man*. Furthermore, like Candide, Joseph Andrews or Gulliver, Jude is also an exemplary or vehicular figure in a tradition that can be traced back to *Everyman* and beyond; a character whose progress has been designed in part as the vehicle of various polemical or satirical arguments about the world's vices and failings. Jude's career has clearly been inflected, time and again, by the author's desire to make critical attacks on social injustice, sexual and religious hypocrisy, and the plight of sensitive beings in an unsympathetic world. Jude sometimes collaborates all too explicitly in this project: then he sermonizes and generalizes with an eloquence more appropriate to the pulpit, the stage or the philosophical treatise than to the mundane conversational milieu of everyday existence.

Yet Jude is also, most of the time, an engagingly plausible and moving literary creation. What makes him engaging is partly his range of evident flaws: if he is a romantic idealist, he is also capable of lust, drunkenness, naïvety and embarrassing folly. If we feel inclined to criticize him, this feeling is largely pre-empted and thereby allayed; for, within the text, he receives innumerable rebukes – from Drusilla, Troutham, Arabella, Tetuphenay, the Artizans' Society, Sue on occasions, the narrator, and repeatedly from himself. The more cogent these criticisms, the more the risk of sentimentality in the characterization (a strong risk, given his sufferings) is reduced. Sometimes he even becomes a blurting figure in a grotesque farce, as when, drunkenly assuring Mr Donn that he is willing to remarry Arabella, he exclaims:

> 'Don't say anything against my honour! . . . . . I'd marry the W— of Babylon rather than do anything dishonourable! No reflection on you, my dear. It is a mere rhetorical figure – what they call in the books, hyperbole.'
>
> 'Keep your figures for your debts . . . . . ,' said Donn.[53]

Another reason for our sympathy is our recognition that Jude is a memorable literary representative of so many forgotten people who have been, and are, 'village Hampdens' and 'mute inglorious Miltons'. Hardy was consciously extending the project of Gray's 'Elegy', to write the history of those ignored by history, and to commemorate the waste of life entailed by economic injustice.

> Chill Penury repressed their noble rage,
> And froze the genial current of the soul.[54]

4.5.3 ARABELLA

The attempt to isolate characters of *Jude the Obscure* for particular consideration induces an informative mental discomfort. This discomfort implies that the characters form a symbiotic system: they interlock in revealing, complementary, contrasting relationships; and the contrasts are qualified by resemblances.

Sue and Arabella are fruitfully contrasted yet complementary; they reveal needs in Jude which neither can fully gratify. If Sue is too fey, 'disembodied', sprite-like, elusive and inhibited, Arabella is fleshly, all too fleshly. The very name, 'Arabella Donn', suggests the phrase 'Arable Bella Donna':[55] the 'ploughable' beautiful woman; and 'belladonna' is a poison, deadly nightshade. Her beauty is of the buxom, chubby, frankly sensuous and hedonistic kind; she is appetitive, but with an appetite that is quick to awaken and quick to surfeit. Hardy associates her with the Delilah who ensnares and defeats her Samson; Jude reproaches himself bitterly for having succumbed to the desire which she can intermittently awaken and reawaken. Her wiles and artifices are patent, though Jude is slow-witted in perceiving them: the length of artificial hair, the contrived dimples, the amateurish yet successful guiles of seduction. (Sue has her own subtler seductive modes and wiles: even here, the text implies similarities beneath contrasts.) Arabella is a mixture of earth-mother and slattern, 'natural woman' and urban trickster, Circe and barmaid.

Fickle, scheming, vulgar, gross and ruthless, Arabella is yet a survivor. She may earn grudging respect as a woman who, in a harsh world, uses her wits and her body to survive and thrive. Phillotson is the recipient of her caustic anti-feminist advice:

'There's nothing like bondage and a stone-deaf taskmaster for taming us women. Besides, you've got the laws on your side. Moses knew. Don't you call to mind what he says?'

'Not for the moment, ma'am, I regret to say.'

'Call yourself a schoolmaster! I used to think o't when they read it in church, and I was carrying on a bit. "Then shall the man be guiltless; but the woman shall bear her iniquity." Damn rough on us women; but we must grin and put up wi' it!'[56]

Her very tone (hectoring, mocking) belies her advice: it's obvious that Arabella herself would be prompt to rebel against 'bondage and a stone-deaf taskmaster'.

As this example indicates, her characterization is strong and dependable; her voice is consistent, clearly recognizable and authentic, while that of Phillotson is greyly prosaic, and the voices of Sue and Jude change their registers awkwardly from the intimate to the literary. Arabella elicits from the reader not moral approval so much as ontological engagement, i.e., a relish of her combative vigour. Descendant of Chaucer's Wife of Bath, ancestress of Brecht's Mother Courage, she has a certain fierce gusto, whether in loving or detesting. Even at her harshest, she makes good sense in her own pragmatic terms; and sometimes she voices the criticisms of Jude and Sue that the reader covertly wishes to hear. Certainly, in the scene of the pig-killing, Jude wins our predominant approval, but Arabella's anger is fully convincing:

''Od damn it all!' she cried, 'that ever I should say it! You've over-stuck un! And I telling you all the time –'

'Do be quiet, Arabella, and have a little pity on the creature!'[57]

Of course Jude has been sensitive and humane in attempting to kill the pig rapidly to terminate its agony; but Arabella's tones express the credible exasperation of the working woman who sees labour wasted and profit thrown away by a misplaced, tardy and impractical humanitarianism. Then, later, there's the telling interview with Sue:

'I have told you he is asking me to marry him – to make our natural marriage a legal one,' said Sue, with yet more dignity. 'It was quite by my wish that he didn't the moment I was free.'

'Ah, yes – you are a oneyer too, like myself,' said Arabella, eyeing her visitor with humorous criticism. 'Bolted from your first, didn't you, like me?'

'Good morning! – I must go,' said Sue hastily.[58]

Here the relatively sensitive and refined Sue is attempting to ward off the relatively rough and coarse Arabella, who hopes to win Jude back; so our sympathies probably lie largely with Sue. Yet, in that exchange, the reader's spirits may lift at Arabella's tough colloquialisms ('a oneyer too', 'bolted from your first'). Against Sue's middle-class diction, Arabella's working-class idioms are briskly reductive; and, as Arabella has seen, there are similarities in situation between the two women, however different their temperaments may be.

Sue and Arabella are indeed, in their contrasting ways, 'oneyers': singular individuals who seek their own paths in life. Arabella's flirtatious method (encouraging Jude, drawing away critically, then encouraging him again) resembles a cruder version of Sue's coquettish variability. Additional similarities are that both Arabella and Sue deride Jude's convictions (Arabella scorning his bookishness, Sue mocking his piety); both leave Jude and marry another man (Cartlett and Phillotson respectively) before returning to him; both women are rivals for his loyalty; and both undergo a religious conversion, though Arabella's is short-lived.

In that last quoted passage, Arabella is 'eyeing her visitor with humorous criticism'. In a harsh and often wretched world, Arabella at least brings a note of humour, however abrasive or sceptical. Taking men and discarding them, producing a child and dispatching him by rail like a parcel, bustling about impatiently to make the best of her lot, Arabella in her resilient selfishness has a degree of gusto and fighting spirit which, set against the melancholy and protracted suffering of Phillotson, Jude and Sue, gives her intermittently an almost Falstaffian positive value. Even when she deserts Jude's deathbed to enjoy the festivities and flirt with Vilbert, our sense of her calculated treachery is compounded with a sense that, as ever, she is resourcefully snatching at life's few pleasures; in its ruthless way, it is an affirmation of vitality and a defiance of conventional pieties. While Jude and Sue have tried to defy convention to maintain their ideals of personal liberty, Arabella defies it to maintain her own hedonistic and materialistic identity. And it is she who is given the last, astutely prophetic, words of the novel, when she comments on the 'peace' that Sue claims to have found since leaving Jude for Phillotson:

'She may swear that on her knees to the holy cross upon her necklace till she's hoarse, but it won't be true! . . . . . She's never found peace since she left his arms, and never will again till she's as he is now!'

4.5.4 PHILLOTSON

Again, the characterization of Phillotson is vigorously integrated into that pattern of contrasts and resemblances which is exemplified by the relationship of Arabella to Sue. Phillotson is in some respects an older, slower, staider version of Jude. It is Phillotson who is initially fired with the ambition to go to Christminster and thus become a graduate and an ordained minister; he, like Jude later, meets with disappointment and frustration, and becomes increasingly rebellious against the moral orthodoxies of his age. After his slow liberal enlightenment through his knowledge of Jude and Sue, and after the lonely experience of social ostracism, he eventually, credibly embittered and hardened by experience, becomes the relatively conventional husband that he had earlier chosen not to be. His retreat from independence to conformism is far less dramatic than Sue's, but implies similar warnings about the ideological, social and even biological forces that ensnare the idealist; though perhaps 'idealist' is too strong a word for the well-meaning character of the drab, perplexed, conscientious schoolmaster.

Near the beginning of the novel, when he leaves Marygreen for Christminster, Phillotson's words to the young Jude are richly pregnant with proleptic ironies.

'I sha'n't forget you, Jude,' he said, smiling, as the cart moved off. 'Be a good boy, remember; and be kind to animals and birds, and read all you can. And if ever you come to Christminster remember you hunt me out for old acquaintance' sake.'

'I sha'n't forget you': but when Jude calls on him at Christminster several years later, his response is (of course) 'I don't remember you in the least.'[59] Again, the admonition to 'be kind to animals and birds' soon causes Jude woe: his chastisement by Farmer Troutham for neglecting the crow-scaring, and later his abuse by Arabella for attempting mercifully to kill their pig. Even the injunction 'read all you can' encourages Jude to develop ideas and ideals which will be doomed mainly to frustration. When Jude, as he was enjoined to, seeks and finds Phillotson, he takes Sue with him, and thus unintentionally becomes matchmaker for an unhappy marriage.

One of the most effective, convincing and moving sequences of the novel is that depicting Phillotson's gradual acquiescence in Sue's desire to leave him for Jude. In spite of the pressures of convention, material self-interest (advancement in his career), his own sexual needs and the counsel of his friend Gillingham, Phillotson puts kindness first and lets her go. The price he pays for his liberalism is illustrated deftly: dismissal from his post, for his immorality in condoning supposed adultery; consequent near-poverty and loneliness. In turn, these setbacks are factors which help him to take Sue back at her request, though the possibility grows 'that the reactionary spirit induced by the world's sneers and his own physical wishes would make Phillotson more orthodoxly cruel to her than he had erstwhile been informally and perversely kind.'[60]

Eventually, in a ferocious irony, the long-suffering, exasperated and frustrated Phillotson makes Sue swear on the New Testament to renounce Jude; and he takes Sue to his bed, knowing full well that, for her, sexual intercourse with him is a mortification of the flesh, a grisly penance and a 'fanatic prostitution'. If the remarriage of Jude to Arabella is a sordid Saturnalia, a self-destructive triumph of drunken flesh over considered judgement, the remarriage of Sue to Phillotson is a self-destructive triumph of her perverse religious guilt (coupled with Victorian prejudice and his long-frustrated sexuality) over the kindness and consideration which Phillotson had once, with understated heroism, so well displayed.

In the 1790s, William Blake condemned a religious and marital system which kills emotional spontaneity:

Prisons are built with stones of Law, Brothels with bricks of Religion.

As the caterpiller chooses the fairest leaves to lay her eggs on, so the priest lays his curse on the fairest joys.

> . . . . . Priests in black gowns were walking their rounds,
> And binding with briars my joys & desires.[61]

A kindred indignation underlies the novel's account of Phillotson's remarriage to Sue; but Hardy also felt, as Blake did not, that there was an inherent flaw in virtually all sexual love-relationships: 'Love lives on propinquity, but dies of contact.'[62] Finally, Hardy's idea that woes increase as civilized sensitive awareness evolves is given jocular reductive force by Widow Edlin's comments on Sue's matrimonial scruples:

'Tis time I got back again to Marygreen – sakes if tidden – if this is what the new notions be leading us to! Nobody thought o' being afeard o' matrimony in my time, nor of much else but a cannon-ball or empty cupboard! Why when I and my poor man were married we thought no more o't than of a game o' dibs!'

And later, when Sue submits to her sexual 'duty' with Phillotson, Edlin muses:

'Poor soul! Weddings be funerals 'a b'lieve nowadays. Fifty-five years ago, come Fall, since my man and I married! Times have changed since then!'[63]

The characterization of Phillotson (the 'very civil, honourable liver' whom 'no woman of any niceness can stomach') thus provides one of the most convincing illustrations of a radical Hardeian paradox: intellectual development extends civilized awareness, yet 'thought is a disease of flesh'.

When standing before certain men the philosopher regrets that thinkers are but perishable tissue, the artist that perishable tissue has to think.[64]

4.5.5 LITTLE FATHER TIME

Although it has recently been challenged, there is a clear and long-established critical consensus that the depiction of 'Little Father Time', the son of Jude and Arabella, is a disaster. The following critical comments are quite representative. J. I. M. Stewart says:

The child arrives magnificently in his railway carriage ..... But he scarcely murders his siblings in the closet more effectively than his creator murders him with deadly prose. We hear of 'the quaint and mysterious personality of Father Time,' of 'a boy with an octogenarian face,' of 'this too reflective child' and so on. What we do *not* hear of is so much as the names of the children he kills; instead, we have portentous remarks from Jude about the catastrophe instancing 'the beginning of the coming universal wish not to live.' Pretty well everything is unrealized throughout this dimension of the novel.[65]

Similarly, A. Alvarez, after making some concessions, concludes:

[H]is ominous remarks, desolation, and self-consciously incurable melancholy are so overdone as to seem almost as though Hardy had decided to parody himself. Even the death of the children, and Father Time's appalling note – '*Done because we are too menny*' – is dangerously close to being laughable: a situation so extreme, insisted on so strongly, seems more appropriate to *grand guignol* than to tragedy ..... What he represents was already embodied in fully tragic form in the figure of Jude. There was no way of repeating it without melodrama.[66]

Father Time, the narrator declares, 'was Age masquerading as Juvenility, and doing it so badly that his real self showed through crevices'. It is tempting to say, instead, 'He was Hardy's extreme pessimism masquerading as a character, and doing it so badly that the author showed through crevices.' He resembles, we are told, 'an enslaved and dwarfed

Divinity'; 'A ground swell from ancient years of night seemed now and then to lift the child'; and 'His face is like the tragic mask of Melpomene'. In portentous prose, the narrator assures us that Time has profound insights into life; but his insights consist of unrelieved gloom about life's woes. At the Agricultural Show, when Jude and Sue are happy, his pessimism does indeed seem almost a parody of Hardy's: 'I should like the flowers very very much, if I didn't keep on thinking they'd all be withered in a few days!'[67]

He is introduced, rather contrivedly and implausibly, at a late stage in the novel. As Stewart noted, his siblings are not even named: they appear to enter the narrative partly to permit the author to illustrate the woes faced by impoverished parents who seek accommodation while encumbered with infants, and partly to be victims of Time's despair. They are born, it seems, in order to die. (Given that Sue is supposed to have 'an intellect that sparkled like a star', her continued production of offspring – 'because it is a law of nature' – indicates a peculiar ignorance of the contraceptive sponge, which was quite widely used then.) With the scene of the killing of the siblings and Time's suicide, the novel does indeed become grotesquely melodramatic in its pessimism. Points made more tellingly elsewhere are here made so blatantly, and with such explicit interpretative commentary ('the coming universal wish not to live') as to be counter-productive. That Schopenhauerian side of Hardy which sees human life as a mistake, and which regards offspring as 'Shapes like our own selves hideously multiplied', has found such crudely overt expression as to induce incredulity. Here a shift in mode from realism towards expressionism and symbolism is made jarringly; a propagandist has prevailed over the artist. That artist is present when Jude is described, with subtle irony, as 'bending over the kettle, with his watch in his hand, timing the eggs, so that his back was turned to the little inner chamber where the children lay':[68] thus Jude concentrates on time while turning his back on Time. The propagandist prevails in the crude pathos and overt thematizing of '*Done because we are too menny*'.

Through the depiction of Father Time, Hardy has tended to mystify or obfuscate (by presenting as a general woe of mankind) various problems of hardship and homelessness for which there are practical solutions. If 'affliction makes opposing forces loom anthropomorphous', depression or political diffidence can make local woes loom cosmic. What has often been overlooked, however, is that this pessimistic 'negative mystification' was dialectical: it was an understandable attempt to challenge the 'positive mystification' which was so abundant in Victorian – and particularly Dickensian – treatments of unfortunate children and their deaths. While 'positive mystification' imposes on an event a *consolatory* symbolic or supernatural aura, 'negative mystification' imposes on an event a *discomfiting* symbolic or supernatural aura.

Father Time, who seems prematurely and uncannily aged, brings to mind a famous predecessor: little Paul Dombey, in Dickens's *Dombey and Son*. Paul, we are told, has a 'strange, old-fashioned, thoughtful way', even at the age of five. He looks and talks 'like one of those terrible little Beings in the Fairy tales, who, at a hundred and fifty or two hundred years of age, fantastically represent the children for whom they have been substituted'. Ailing yet stoical, the lad imagines his dead mother waiting for him on that far shore beyond the ocean of death; and eventually, while he embraces his devoted sister Florence, his life draws to its close in a vision of heaven:

> Presently he told her that the motion of the boat upon the stream was lulling him to rest. How green the banks were now, how bright the flowers growing on them, and how tall the rushes! Now the boat was out at sea, but gliding smoothly on. And now there was a shore before him. Who stood on the bank! –
> . . . . . 'Mamma is like you, Floy. I know her by the face! But tell them that the print [of Jesus] upon the stairs at school is not divine enough. The light about the head is shining on me as I go!' . . . . .
> O thank GOD . . . . . for that older fashion yet, of Immortality! And look upon us, angels of young children, with regards not quite estranged, when the swift river bears us to the ocean![69]

It forms a characteristically religiose death-scene for a Dickensian youngster. In *Oliver Twist*, 'Little Dick' had looked forward to Heaven and its angels; in *Nicholas Nickleby*, Smike has visions of the beautiful heavenly gardens in which there are many children 'with light upon their faces'; in *The Old Curiosity Shop*, Little Nell resembles 'angels in their majesty' in her death; and, in *Bleak House*, Jo's poignant death is accompanied by a reading of the Lord's Prayer. Hardy's treatment of the suicide of Father Time after the killing of the siblings is, in part, a sceptic's sardonic counter-attack on that tradition of the religiose and largely sentimental treatment of the mortality of youngsters. Father Time is young-old and prematurely wise, like Paul Dombey; but whereas Paul sees his mother and Jesus awaiting him on the far shore, Time, having seen the terrors of life, expires with 'glazed eyes . . . . . slanted into the room'.

Part 5 Critical Viewpoints

The first four sections of this part offer a selection of critical comments on *Jude the Obscure* which spans a century, from the 1890s to the 1990s; and the fifth section reappraises various problems of the text in the light of those comments.

5.1 Contemporaneous Comments

The earliest reviews of *Jude the Obscure* were numerous and often lengthy; and the range of judgement was remarkable. At one extreme were reviewers who damned the book for its immorality and coarseness; at the opposite extreme were reviewers who acclaimed it as a great and truthful work; and between them were those who offered a mixed, qualified account.[1]

Mrs Oliphant, in *Blackwood's Magazine*, found the book full of 'grossness, indecency, and horror':

There may be books more disgusting, more impious as regards human nature, more foul in detail, in those dark corners where the amateurs of filth find garbage to their taste; but not, we repeat, from any Master's hand.

In particular, some of the scenes involving Arabella are 'more brutal in their depravity than anything which the darkest slums could bring forth'. Jude, instead of lamenting his lot, should have 'shown himself superior to the lower animals' by resisting his desire for Arabella. As for the deaths of Jude's children:

Mr. Hardy's solution of the great insoluble question of what is to be the fate of children in such circumstances brings this nauseous tragedy suddenly and at a stroke into the region of pure farce . . . . .

An unsigned review in the *Athenaeum* declared, 'here we have a titanically bad novel', and argued (shrewdly) that Hardy is tempted to envisage fate not as a blind force but as a spiteful one:

The way it is done is extremely simple: you take a man with good aspirations – a weak man he must be, of course – and put down to his credit all his aspirations and the feeble attempts he makes to realize them, while all the mistakes he makes, which render his life a failure, you put down to the savage deity who lies in wait to trip him up.

Jude and Sue asked for trouble by living together unmarried; having chosen to defy society, 'it is absurd of them to repine'. The plot, in the contrivance of the double remarriage, 'makes the whole book appear dangerously near to farce'; the dialogue is sometimes implausibly didactic; and Jude is made to suffer so that 'Mr. Hardy may rage furiously'. Nevertheless, even this reviewer found time to praise the depiction of the rural background and of the minor characters.

The *Pall Mall Gazette* referred to the novel as 'Jude the Obscene', summarized it facetiously, and asked the author to supply a 'cleaner' book, 'to take the bad taste out of our mouths'. This reviewer, like several others, was clearly offended by the scene of the children's deaths. The *Spectator* found it too offensive to be reviewed, declaring that Hardy and Grant Allen were propagandists for an immoral 'new morality': '*Jude the Obscure* is too deplorable a falling-off from Mr. Hardy's former achievements to be reckoned with at all.' The *Fortnightly Review* declared it 'a dismal treatise' in which Hardy 'is depressing because he is himself somewhat depressed', and criticized the implausibly pedantic dialogues of Jude and Sue.

The main defences of the novel came, predictably, from relatively radical or 'advanced' magazines. The *Saturday Review* claimed that the sexual matter which had so annoyed intemperate critics was secondary; what counted mainly was that 'For the first time in English literature the almost intolerable difficulties that beset an ambitious man of the working class . . . . . receive adequate treatment'. This is the 'most splendid' of Hardy's works. For the *Westminster Review*, it was so moving a novel as to confirm that Hardy 'is the greatest living English writer of fiction'; and the *Free Review* found it, in its realism and poignancy, 'the supreme achievement of a great artist' – an opinion echoed by Richard le Gallienne in *The Idler*. Havelock Ellis (*Savoy Magazine*) offered a lengthy defence of *Jude* against its detractors, praising its realism:

In *Jude the Obscure* we find for the first time in our literature the reality of marriage clearly recognized as something wholly apart from the mere ceremony with which our novelists have usually identified it.

Edmund Gosse, in another lengthy and measured appraisal (in *Cosmopolis*) found the story 'ghastly' in summary, the dialogue marred by jargon, and the tone sometimes too strident:

What has Providence done to Mr. Hardy that he should rise up in the arable land of Wessex and shake his fist at his Creator?

Yet the power, vigour and vividness of the achievement remain un-doubted, Gosse declared. '*Jude the Obscure* is an irresistible book.'

Meanwhile, American reviews displayed much the same range, extend-ing from disgust and revulsion to high praise for its tragic power. Undoubtedly, the extent of the controversy was itself a selling-point; and, in the subsequent decades, there were few critical verdicts which had not been anticipated in the ample range of those early appraisals.

5.2 D. H. Lawrence's *Study of Thomas Hardy*

From time to time, novelists and critics have exposed themselves to the mockery of posterity by the patronizing tones in which they have spoken of Hardy. Henry James, for instance, remarked:

The good little Thomas Hardy has scored a great success with *Tess of the d'Urbervilles*, which is chock-full of faults and falsity and yet has a singular beauty and charm . . . . .

But oh yes . . . . ., she is vile. The pretence of 'sexuality' is only equalled by the absence of it, and the abomination of the language by the author's reputation for style. There are indeed some pretty smells and sights and sounds. But you have better ones in Polynesia. [2]

In 1934, T. S. Eliot, in his notorious *After Strange Gods*, spoke of Hardy as a decadent provincial writer who was 'indifferent even to the prescripts of good writing'.[3] Perhaps the oddest lukewarm estimate was that by F. R. Leavis, who, in *The Great Tradition* (1948), quoted with approval James's remarks about the 'good little Thomas Hardy' and added:

This concedes by implication all that properly can be conceded – unless we claim more for *Jude the Obscure*, which, of all Hardy's works of a major philosophic-tragic ambition, comes nearer [*sic*] to sustaining it, and, in its clumsy way – which hasn't the rightness with which the great novelists show their profound sureness of their essential purpose – is impressive . . . . .

[B]y the side of George Eliot . . . . . Hardy, decent as he is, [seems] a provincial manufacturer of gauche and heavy fictions that sometimes have corresponding virtues.[4]

While Leavis granted a chapter of his book to George Eliot, and later devoted a whole enthusiastic volume to D. H. Lawrence, Hardy was thus relegated, even though it can be argued that Hardy's novels con-stitute a most important linkage between the George Eliot of *Middle-march* and the D. H. Lawrence of *The Rainbow* and *Women in Love*. Indeed, much of Lawrence's writing can be seen as a creative quarrel with Hardy, on Hardy's own ground: the interaction of rural and urban life during the great transition from the mid-Victorian to the early modern era; the relationship of new knowledge to old beliefs; and that 'deadly war waged between flesh and spirit'. The relationship of Lawrence to Hardy can be seen as that of a brilliantly rebellious son to a powerfully provocative father.

The most explicit evidence for this claim is Lawrence's book-length *Study of Thomas Hardy*, written in 1914 and published posthumously in *Phoenix* [I], 1936. Here Lawrence develops at length his thesis that the basis of human ideology over thousands of years has been the dialectical struggle between, on the one hand, a female principle, which he associates with nature, law, senses, feelings and (paradoxically) God the Father, and, on the other hand, a male principle, which he associates with love, spirit, mind and Jesus the Son. Hardy's works, Lawrence argues, constitute a graphic illustration of this ages-old struggle. For instance:

Jude is only Tess turned round about. Instead of the heroine containing the two principles, male and female, at strife within her one being, it is Jude who contains them both, whilst the two women with him take the place of the two men to Tess. Arabella is Alec d'Urberville, Sue is Angel Clare. These represent the same pair of principles.[5]

Hardy, according to Lawrence's thesis, is an inwardly divided artist. Any work of art 'must contain the essential criticism of the morality to which it adheres'; so, while Hardy intends to denigrate the body and the physical, his texts reveal a deep 'sensuous understanding' which subverts that intention. We see that 'Arabella was, under all her disguise of pig-fat, and false hair, and vulgar speech, in character somewhat of an aristocrat'; she 'makes a man' of Jude; he 'becomes a grown, independent man in the arms of Arabella'; she 'made him free'. As for Sue:

She was born with the vital female atrophied in her: she was almost male. Her *will* was male. It was wrong for Jude to take her physically, it was a violation of her. She was not the virgin type, but the witch type, which has no sex . . . . .[6]

She is almost pure consciousness, and she awakens Jude to full mental being. Their tragedy is that Jude demands a sexual response which is alien to her nature; he effectively violates her, and is drained rather than fulfilled as a result. It is inevitable that the children die, since Sue was not meant to have children in the first place. If Jude and Sue never marry, it is because 'they knew it was no marriage; they knew it was wrong, all along; they knew they were sinning against life, in forcing a physical marriage between themselves'. If they are instinctively disliked by other people, it is because the others sense that they have thus sinned against life. Their real marriage was 'in the roses'. Finally,

this tragedy is the result of over-development of one principle of human life at the expense of the other; an over-balancing; a laying of all stress on the Male, the Love, the Spirit, the Mind, the Consciousness; a denying, a blaspheming against the Female, the Law, the Soul, the Senses, the Feelings.[7]

Eventually, Lawrence suggests, both in literature and at large there may be a reconciliation of Law and Love, Father and Son, feelings and mind.

His account of Thomas Hardy is rich, vivid, provocative. In its emphasis on divided intentions within the creative imagination, the *Study* anticipates many later critics – structuralists, deconstructionists, cultural materialists – who emphasized and exaggerated the importance of detecting contradictions within literary texts. Even when Lawrence seems perverse in his assessments, there is something within the novel which provides evidence. For example, he may seem perverse in suggesting that Arabella is an 'aristocrat' who liberates Jude's manhood, for Hardy emphasizes that Arabella is a vulgar schemer who ensnares her victim. Yet, as we have seen, the characterization of Arabella does contain countervailing traits; she may not be a natural aristocrat, but she does have a tough vitality and resilience which sometimes contrast tellingly with the nervous intellectualism of Sue. Again, though Hardy might predominantly have intended us to see Jude as a potential scholar and intellectual who is sadly denied fulfilment, part of the text indeed questions the value of such intellectual aspirations. Here Hardy's element of cultural primitivism[8] resembles Lawrence's. The narrator of the novel remarks that 'Sarcophagus College' exudes 'gloom, bigotry, and decay', and he says of Jude:

For a moment there fell on Jude a true illumination; that here in the stone yard was a centre of effort as worthy as that dignified by the name of scholarly study within the noblest of the colleges . . . . .

It would have been far better for him in every way if he had never come within sight and sound of the delusive precincts . . . . .

He saw that his destiny lay not with these, but among the manual toilers in the shabby purlieu which he himself occupied, unrecognized as part of the city at all by its visitors and panegyrists, yet without whose denizens the hard readers could not read nor the high thinkers live.[9]

For all this, Lawrence seems, finally, to be converting *Jude the Obscure* into a more Lawrentian novel than Hardy wrote; for Hardy's distrust of the instincts, of the flesh, is more sustained and radical than Lawrence's interpretation suggests; and Hardy seeks to blame nature, heredity, society and institutions, rather than any life-denial by Sue and Jude, for their downfall.

In fact, much of the discussion of *Jude* in the *Study of Thomas Hardy* brings a different yet strongly related novel to mind. That novel is Lawrence's *Women in Love*, which was being written at the same time as the *Study*. What is said of Jude often evokes a memory of Birkin; the account of Sue brings Gudrun to mind. In *Women in Love*, Lawrence extends the debates of *Jude the Obscure*: the debates about the pressures exerted on the self by modernity, industrialism, urbanization, cultural scepticism; about the antagonism of 'Law' and 'Love', instinct and intellect; about the value and perils of education; about the deracinated condition of modern intellectuals from provincial England.

The central contrast is that whereas Hardy, the post-Darwinian, often saw nature as dauntingly indifferent or as a cruel battleground in which humans were reluctant participants and dismayed spectators, Lawrence, the anti-Darwinian, saw nature as a cosmic life-force to which humans might healingly attune themselves. Hardy saw nature as a senseless trap for 'unnecessary' sentient lives; Lawrence saw it as a source of refuge and healing, to which humans might escape from the trap of life-denying 'mental consciousness'. Hardy was bitterly aware of snared rabbits, slaughtered pigs and caged birds; Lawrence envisaged the bower of Sherwood Forest as an Edenic location of love and harmony.

Yet, for all the transvaluation effected by Lawrence, for all the contrast offered by his sense of cosmic vitality to Hardy's sense of cosmic fatality, the continuities remain. The sense of characterization as location of paradox, contradiction, struggle and fluctuation – that is keenly present in both writers. In descriptions, they display a kindred sense of scenic montage; they like situations in which two or three characters and an animal or other central object are seen both realistically and symbolically – Jude, Arabella and the pig; Gudrun, Gerald and his mare; Jude, Sue and the roses; Gudrun, Gerald and the lilies; Jude, Sue and the snared rabbit; Gerald, Gudrun and the terrified rabbit. In their writings, the range of reference constantly reaches out, far beyond the present moment of closely observed encounters to the remote reaches of history or space or time. Both writers protest against the fetters imposed by conventional morality; both demand greater sexual liberty;

both, while deeply preoccupied by religious ways of appraising the world, oppose the established Church's taboos, denials and repressions. In both writers, language itself is richly paradoxical; both offer protagonists (Jude, Birkin, Tess, Mellors) who shift between the rural vernacular and an educated middle-class vocabulary; and both imply the value and limitations of each mode of discourse. Even in their didactic explications and satiric bitternesses, the narrators in Hardy and Lawrence display kindred impatience.

In short, the *Study of Thomas Hardy* offers some insights into Hardy, many into Lawrence; and, above all, it dramatically illustrates the way in which literature evolves by dialectical struggle. Lawrence learned much from Hardy; there is emulation, rivalry and a fierce dispute between them about the valuation of evolution, of nature, of human instincts and human consciousness.

5.3 Marxist and Related Views

Apart from the requirement to indicate approval of Marx and of social revolution which liberates the workers, there has been little agreement about what should constitute a Marxist approach to literature. Critics who deem themselves Marxists have adopted conflicting approaches (formalism, socialist realism, structuralism, post-structuralism, etc.) and have been assailed by other critics who purport to be Marxists. Given that both the theory and the practice of Marxism have been anti-democratic, the readiness of numerous western literary critics to commend Marxism while personally enjoying the relative freedom of life in a democratic system holds marked irony. Such critics tend to define 'ideology' pejoratively, and to talk as though the particular writer under their scrutiny is subject to ideology; yet they tend also to imply that they themselves transcend the grip of ideology. The reader may well reflect that if the critic can transcend ideology, so may the writer; or that if ideology is all-embracing, it must embrace the critic too; or that if a conflict of ideologies provides opportunities for relatively independent thought, those opportunities may be exploited by the author as well as by his critic.

In practice, Marxist commentators on Hardy predictably emphasized and extended the critical procedure (already well established by critics as diverse as Pope, Johnson, Blake, Hazlitt, Beerbohm and Lawrence) of seeking tensions, contradictions and lacunae within the texts under consideration. These features they regarded as the outcome of ideological divisions inevitably generated by class conflicts within society. In *Criticism and Ideology* (1976), Terry Eagleton declared:

Ambiguously placed within both his own declining rural enclave and the social formation at large ....., Hardy's situation as a literary producer was ridden with contradictions.[10]

Earlier Marxist critics, notably Lukács and his followers who pilloried Brecht, had strongly favoured realism; but later Marxist critics preferred to regard realism as a 'bourgeois' mode which buttressed middle-class assumptions. (Such academic critics, though patently of the middle class themselves, commonly spoke of the middle class or 'bourgeoisie' in such a derogatory way as to imply that they themselves were superior to it.) One consequence was that Hardy's notorious breaches of realism – the coincidental plotting, melodramatic incidents, etc. – were now seen not as regrettable signs of incompetence but rather as laudable signs of ideological revolt against realism and its supposedly conservative tendencies. Accordingly, Eagleton said of *Jude the Obscure*:

What have been read as its 'crudities' are less the consequence of some artistic incapacity than of an astonishing raw boldness on Hardy's part, a defiant flouting of 'verisimilitude' which mounts theatrical gesture upon gesture in a driving back of the bounds of realism.[11]

George Wotton's *Thomas Hardy: Towards a Materialist Criticism* (1985) developed at length a kindred thesis. Failing to note the damaging self-contradictions in Marx (whom he cited frequently and approvingly), Wotton offered an elaborate discussion of Hardy's ideological contradictions which contained various interesting notions. For example:

In the last analysis, what Hardy's writing 'cannot see' is its own place and function in the class structure it is at such pains to reveal. While ceaselessly producing images of class conflict it denies the necessity of class struggle by 'revealing' it to be the concealing inessential form which must be stripped away in order that essential reality – the true realities of life – can be revealed and *take its place*. I say what Hardy's writing cannot see rather than what Hardy cannot see because this is not a matter of the writer's conscious intention but rather of the determinations operated by the writing's ideological means of production, especially those 'harmonizing' discourses which attempted to resolve the material contradictions of class society by 'doing away' with classes.[12]

Wotton explains that whereas traditional literary criticism treats writing as a coded message to be deciphered, 'materialist criticism treats it as an object of knowledge and seeks to elaborate the conditions of its production'.[13] Traditional criticism has actually *constructed* the 'faults' of Hardy's writing: by conspiring to see stylistic infelicities, uneven workmanship and improbable plots, the literary establishment has been displaying a form of snobbery linked to a conservative taste for realism and for the image of Hardy as a provincial.

It is important and necessary to understand that the Thomas Hardy who exists in the discourses and material practices which form the apparatus of the cultural hegemony of the ruling class is the construction of an ideological discourse which maintains the deep social divisions in our society.[14]

(Sue anticipated Wotton in plainer terms when she described Christminster as 'a nest of commonplace schoolmasters whose characteristic is timid obsequiousness to tradition'.)[15] In short, the vast majority of teachers and literary critics who discuss Thomas Hardy are part of the great cultural conspiracy by the 'ruling class' to conserve its position; and, indeed, Hardy himself, as traditionally perceived, has been made into another buttress of that class. Instead of 'constructing' the faults of Thomas Hardy, Wotton (who himself, it follows, is a cultural construction) prefers to construct the faults of the 'ruling class'.

The theory that Hardy has been recruited by bourgeois critics and the media into an unconscious conspiracy to make people conservative was developed further by Peter Widdowson's *Hardy in History: A Study in Literary Sociology* (1989). The villain of Widdowson's book is the bourgeois 'liberal-humanist' outlook, which allegedly values conventional realism and seeks to depict Hardy as 'a great modern tragic humanist and rural annalist'. Against that outlook, Widdowson advocates a 'cultural materialism' indebted to Marx, who is repeatedly cited uncritically. (Wotton and Eagleton are also acknowledged.) The logic of the book often appears to be that of 'two wrongs making one right': since Hardy has been 'appropriated' by forces deemed conservative, Widdowson will seek to appropriate him for the benefit of Marxism – not by claiming that Hardy was some kind of Marxist, but by claiming that the texts permit far more subversive readings than they have generally received.

Propounding a familiar paradox, Widdowson suggests that the *Life of Thomas Hardy* (ostensibly by F. E. Hardy) is 'fiction presented as fact': by its silences, evasions and distortions, this work reveals the conflicting social and ideological pressures in Hardy's life. For example, Hardy disclaims social ambition and is often critical of the socially high, yet he loves to list the titled and distinguished people whom he met. He seeks to depict himself as apolitical, because he is able neither 'to follow a "socialistic" logic because of his newly-acquired social status' nor 'to accept the conventional political, social and religious orthodoxies of the ruling class'.

The Life ..... is both one of Hardy's fictions and complicit in the construction of 'Hardy' as the essentially apolitical, 'disinterested', tragic poet and man of letters ..... [16]

If the *Life* is best seen as a disguised work of fiction, the early novel *The Hand of Ethelberta* is best seen as a disguised autobiography. Widdowson ingeniously argues that this largely neglected and disparaged work, dealing with a woman who successfully climbs socially by means of her skills as a storyteller, offers a mockingly self-reflexive narrative. Here Hardy reveals the price (in terms of social subterfuges, alienation and self-repression) exacted by literary success. *The Hand of Ethelberta* discloses 'the alienating and destructive processes of a class society'.

What it suggests, surely, is that the matrix in which Hardy's contradictory fictional discourses are shaped is composed of his insecurities and fears about class and gender, and that this permits the consciousness of the novels to 'perceive' the very conditioning it is itself subject to.[17]

By considering at length these supposedly revealing qualities of *The Hand of Ethelberta*, Widdowson makes two tactical moves simultaneously. First, he challenges the 'canonical' view that whereas the five novels of 'character and environment' are the great achievements, the remaining novels of Hardy can safely be relegated as manifestly inferior works. Second, he challenges the critical preference for the 'realistic' Hardy by advocating the merits of a text which is manifestly 'artificial' and concerned with literary 'artifice'. Since realism aids and abets liberal humanism (he alleges), Marxist critics and their allies should become advocates of the anti-realistic feature of Hardy's writing.

For example, the extraordinary set of coincidences which result in Mrs Yeobright's death in *The Return of the Native* no longer appear as the creaking mechanism of 'plot as fate', but as a structural metaphor for the inescapably contingent relations the 'metamorphic' characters of that novel find themselves in. Again, the 'improbable' presentation of Little Father Time in *Jude the Obscure* and his death with the other children – '"Done because we are too menny"' – becomes in itself a formal demystification of the illusory fictions of realism and humanism.[18]

Thus Hardy is not merely 'straining at the limits of "probablist" realist discourse' but is 'strategically anti-realist'.

In these accounts by Eagleton, Wotton and Widdowson there is much that is helpful and much that is suspect. Their disparagement of the 'liberal humanist' or 'bourgeois' tradition implies disparagement of the democratic tradition which liberalism has nurtured; and their advocacy of Marxism or 'materialism' entails support for an anti-democratic tradition which is now historically discredited. Their theory of the 'unconscious conspiracy' of critics and teachers to impose conservative interpretations on Hardy understates the diversity of available readings and implies the élitist notion that while the many are blinded by indoctrination, a select few (the 'materialist' critics and their allies) are permitted to see what is objectively the case. The notion that realism and conservatism go hand in hand is false, given not only the diversity of progressive social criticisms voiced in realist texts but also the fact that some anti-realist texts (notably Eliot's *The Waste Land* and Pound's *Cantos*) have been the vehicles of markedly right-wing ideas. If it be argued that in the case of Eliot's and Pound's poems, the ideas are subverted by the implications of the form, one obvious response is that a symmetrical logic could be used to defend realism: if the form has conservative implications (which is not necessarily the case), those implications might be subverted by the ideas expressed.

Nevertheless, when allowance has been made for such suspect features in their arguments, these 'materialist' critics have provided a range of useful challenges. By stressing the ways in which both Hardy's writing and its subsequent reception have been 'sites of struggle' in which 'aesthetic' considerations are inseparable from social and political considerations, they effectively extended the territory of discussion. At their best, they indeed seemed to be explicating what Hardy's fiction, in its tensions, anxieties and contortions, seems to be implying. In *Jude the Obscure*, Jude's children perished in a closet, but in cultural history he might seem to have descendants among those 'materialists' of the late twentieth century who protested against the 'social moulds'. Jude, however, regarded 'class-feeling' (like 'patriotism, save-your-own-soul-ism, and other virtues') as 'a mean exclusiveness at bottom'.[19]

5.4 Feminist Views

Kate Millett's *Sexual Politics* (1970) rejuvenated feminist studies of literature: fierce, concise, widely ranging, sometimes unfair but eminently quotable, her controversial study changed the agenda of literary discussions by emphasizing the extent of sexist assumptions and stereotypes in works of and around the literary canon.

Jude the Obscure emerged with considerable credit from Millett's inquisition. There were strong qualifications, of course. Jude's consciousness is fully presented (Millett argued), whereas Sue's is not; Jude's characterization is firm and clear, Sue's is rather a muddle – now convincing, now unconvincing. Hardy makes Sue a compound of New Woman, lily with a brain, Frigid Woman – she is by turns 'an enigma, a pathetic creature, a nut, and an iceberg'; yet 'quite the finest thing in the book is his sensitive, perceptive account of Sue's capitulation'. This novel, says Millett, helps the feminist 'sexual revolution' in three ways:

[F]irst, ... its savage criticism of institutions – marriage and sexual ownership – its impassioned plea for divorce . . . . . Secondly, Hardy is to be commended for creating in Sue an intelligent rebel against sexual politics and in [*sic*] understanding the forces which defeat such a rebel. Finally, the novel's greatest fascination resides in its demonstration of how very difficult such a revolution can be – not only for its participants but even for the author who would describe it. *Jude the Obscure* is on very solid ground when attacking the class system, but when it turns to the sexual revolution, Hardy himself is troubled and confused. [20]

This last charge was explicitly challenged by Mary Jacobus in the essay 'Sue the Obscure' (1975). For Jacobus, the character of Sue is centrally clear:

The central aspect of Sue's character is not that in her the female is atrophied . . . . . but that in her the individual is highly developed. [21]

Sue tries to maintain her independence; there is some regret in her acquiescence in Jude's sexual insistence; but her consequent shared sexual happiness with him is plain from the way in which she kisses Jude 'in a way she had never done before' and in the communion with the roses at the agricultural show.

The roses are indeed symbolic, as Lawrence asserts – but they are symbolic of more than spiritual communion. The rose which complements the lily in Sue has been brought into flower by Jude; it is he who gives her the playful push into contact with her own sensuous nature, making her fully and joyously responsive here. [22]

Repeatedly, Jacobus insists that the characterization of Sue is coherent and plausible: Sue's tragedy is that she who strove so hard to guard her independence is defeated by bitter experience – of men, of sexuality, of society, and of nature.

The death of the children is the most flagrant instance of Hardy's preparedness to sacrifice verisimilitude to his diagrammatic design, but we are never allowed to forget that *Jude* is a novel of contrasting ideas. The culminating and most crucial of them is that between Sue's unbalance and Jude's disillusion. Throughout the book, however, the rigid ironies of Hardy's scheme have been translated into the changing consciousness of his characters. Hence the unexpected effect of a novel at once fixed and fluid, over-emphatic and true to life. Events which seem contrived precipitate inner changes which are painfully authenticated. The peculiar modernity of *Jude* lies in the weight it gives to such changes.[23]

Jude dies defiant, 'Samson-like, not only in his weakness for women, but in his final strength of purpose'; but finally, 'Sue's tormented consciousness haunts us more than Jude's bitter oblivion'.[24]

Three years later, Gail Cunningham's *The New Woman and the Victorian Novel* related *Jude the Obscure* to the large context of debate about the 'New Woman' of the late nineteenth century; and, as we have seen, Cunningham argued that Sue is a hybrid characterization, insufficiently resolved:

[The novel's] main themes and ideas are sketched out with reasonable clarity, but are not filled in with sufficient supportive evidence, or else become blurred by conflicting reports on the characters, particularly Sue . . . . . In Sue more than in any of the other heroines we feel Hardy's conception of women pulling against his desire to expound theories about social organisation.[25]

Sue may voice revolt against convention, but her brief period of success (in her happy months with Jude) is too sketchily presented, and her collapse into 'crushing conformity' is a characteristic of much fiction dealing with the New Woman. Thus Hardy is divided between approval of Sue's protest and a conventional desire to demonstrate that such pride leads to downfall.

John Goode, however, in 'Sue Bridehead and the New Woman' (1979), assailed the idea that the presentation of Sue is inconsistent. Goode cites Bathsheba's claim in *Far from the Madding Crowd*: 'It is difficult for a woman to define her feelings in language which is chiefly made by men to express theirs.'

What makes Sue effective is her function in the novel, which is the function of an exposing image – that is to say, of an image carrying its own logic which is not the logic of the understandable, comprising both what she utters and what she seems, the gap between them and the collusion they make . . . . . [W]hat makes for her coherence is neither her consistency nor Hardy's, but the persistent way in which she exposes the limits of meaning.[26]

Thus Sue's enigmatic complexity reveals the attempts of ideology to impose conventional identities on women.

Goode's point was partly endorsed by Penny Boumelha (in *Thomas Hardy and Women*, 1982), who contested A. O. J. Cockshut's claim that *Jude the Obscure* refutes feminist thought by showing Sue's failure to overcome woman's natural limitations. On the contrary:

Sue's 'breakdown' is not the sign of some gender-determined constitutional weakness of mind or will, but a result of the fact that certain social forms press harder on women in sexual and marital relationships, largely by virtue of the implication of their sexuality in child-bearing.[27]

The failure of the attempt by Jude and Sue to live together outside convention shows us

the economic and ideological pressures which wrench the relationship back into pre-determined forms of marriage, just as Hardy's novel is wrenched back finally into pre-existing fictional forms; but it is part of the strength of *Jude* that it makes visible the violence of those wrenchings, and gives a sense of the energy which cannot be wholly contained within those forms.[28]

Rosemarie Morgan's *Women and Sexuality in the Novels of Thomas Hardy* (1988) took issue with the claim advanced by Mary Jacobus that Jude and Sue do achieve a period of mutual joy and sexual fulfilment. Whereas Jude, the morning after copulating with Sue, is 'gaily' planning marriage, Sue is subdued and preoccupied: the text states that 'a glow had passed away from her and depression sat upon her features'. Sue has been coerced into sexual intercourse by Jude's frustration, irritation and recriminations; and she is bound to experience guilt and depression subsequently, because Jude has idealized her as a noble being free from 'grossness':

In high-ranking her over the sexual act, in denying her a sexual reality, in nullifying her needs and desires, Jude unwittingly enforces her subjugation.[29]

Morgan's thesis was developed and modified by Phillip Mallett in 'Sexual Ideology and Narrative Form in *Jude the Obscure*' (1989). According to Mallett, Jude and Sue are alike victims of ideological dualisms:

The dominant language of the book, then, though it is not one that is *approved* in the novel, privileges, or appears to privilege one set of terms over another: spirit, soul, noble, high, etc., over flesh, body, gross, low, etc., and in the process suggests that whatever the ostensible topic of their discussions – religious belief, academic aims, sexual behaviour – Jude and Sue will have to encounter the same all-pervading dualism . . . . . [T]he values of society are not 'out there', distinct from the consciousness of Jude and Sue, but permeate their language and their being.[30]

Sue thus finds herself in an intolerable position: 'sexual love is "nothing", and it is everything; it is "gross", and it is the mark of an ultimate commitment . . . . .' Hardy's strategy, therefore, is to expose the coercive functions of language:

[H]e explores the clash of languages around Sue, within which her identity is constructed, but does not pretend to offer a 'meta-language' granting direct access to her being.[31]

Furthermore, this scepticism about language entails scepticism about the very nature of the novel itself. By various devices, notably the numerous epigraphs and quotations in the text, Hardy emphasizes the novel's fictionality.

The language of the fiction, like the language of sexual identity, is being exposed as made, not given, the novel, that is to say, is not presented as a revelation, an uncovering of what is demonstrably 'there', but confesses itself the result of human action: imperfect, therefore, and implicated in those forms of language in which Sue is seen to be entrapped. Through its interruptions, silences and juxtapositions, the narrative form of the novel dramatises and echoes the predicament of its heroine.[32]

The present reader will notice that, at this point, the discussion of feminist aspects of *Jude the Obscure* reflects that distrust of realist fiction and that delight in sceptical 'deconstruction' which was illustrated by the Marxist critics previously cited here, and which indeed is one of the identifying characteristics of literary criticism in the late twentieth century. If, a century previously, a dominant fashion in criticism was the asking of the question 'Is this text morally laudable?', the subsequent fashion has been to ask 'Is this text politically "progressive" in its scepticism about literature and about language itself?' Similarly, the question 'Is this work an organic whole, a harmonious unity?' has been displaced by the question 'Does this work have interesting divisions, gaps or contradictions?' Repeatedly in the late twentieth century, critics have praised texts which, in their view, reveal that fiction is merely fiction and that conventions of language powerfully influence our understanding of reality. Never before has so much critical ingenuity been devoted to demonstrating what has long been known. Critics often present as recent knowledge various sceptical ideas formulated during many past centuries by Pyrrho, Hobbes, Hume, Nietzsche and numerous other philosophers. Marxists and feminists have often forgotten that linguistic scepticism is no more left-wing than right-wing in its consequences. Nietzsche, who claimed that 'Truths are illusions of which we have forgotten that they are illusions', [33] was anti-feminist and anti-socialist. Furthermore, if Hardy indicates discrepancies between language and reality, he necessarily does so by representing *in language* that discrepant reality. Jude and Phillotson are tantalized, aroused and baffled by Sue's elusiveness; but her indefinability itself is well defined; and innumerable descriptive details give her a memorable distinctiveness. Physically, in her slender figure, her tremulous voice, her lithe movement, her light walk, Hardy creates an identifiable embodied personality. Sue could be recognized instantly in the street; and aspects of her can be recognized today in many real women.

5.5 Retrospect: Sue, Time, Structure, Language

5.5.1 THE DEPICTION OF SUE

That critics should take such widely divergent views of Sue is fully understandable, given the designed complexity of her character and career. She is in part, designedly, enigmatic and variable, a strange compound even to herself: the text makes this explicit. The flow of authorial sympathy moves to and fro around her. Her characterization is also crowded by the numerous illustrative functions that Hardy wishes it to hold.

As we noted previously, Hardy's ambivalence about sexual desire leads him in various directions. First, the Sue who is resistant to men's regular sexual demands can be seen as a sensitive, refined, highly evolved person, persistently being harassed by the 'coarse' needs of masculinity; she can think of the loss of her virginity as 'amputation'. Yet she can also be seen, and sometimes regards herself, as one who flirtatiously aroused such desire and who, by subsequent denial, tormented the men around her: she 'loves to be loved' and to exercise the power of her attractiveness. When she first submits sexually to Jude, we are indeed told that the next morning she is a saddened, crestfallen figure. Yet, as time passes and she becomes inured to living with Jude, becoming repeatedly pregnant, we are assured that she has entered a 'dream paradise' with him. Later, after the children's deaths, she experiences the bitter revulsion and guilt.

The characterization may be regarded as supporting the feminist cause in the following ways; but each way has a critical corollary.

First, Sue (until her recantation) speaks eloquently for those women who resent the masculine assumption that the female, whether wife or mistress, should regularly comply with the male partner's sexual demands. However, an objection in this case is that Hardy is drawing on a conventional Victorian notion that the sensitive, 'refined' female is sexually reluctant and reticent; indeed, Sue suggests that the 'average woman' is superior to the 'average man' in that 'she never instigates, only responds' (which, if true, places Arabella in a 'low' category of exceptional instigators).

Second: Sue can be seen as a representative of women who wish to preserve their independence of character in a world which variously coerces women to adopt stereotypical and submissively conventional roles. Here the complication is that her attempt to preserve independence is linked to that quality of apparent coquetry which she defines thus:

I did not exactly flirt with you; but that inborn craving which undermines some women's morals almost more than unbridled passion – the craving to attract and captivate, regardless of the injury it may do the man – was in me . . . . . [H]owever it ended, it began in the selfish and cruel wish to make your heart ache for me without letting mine ache for you.[34]

(She is capable of explaining that 'men are – so much better than women!')[35]

Third: Sue is intellectually emancipated, a bright inquirer and challenger of a largely patriarchal system, understandably resistant to the institution of marriage, understandably aware that the social moulds provided by society are inadequate vehicles for the diversity of individual lives. Here one complication, as we have noted, is that an ideal she envisages (an ideal contemplated by Phillotson too) is of a family unit consisting only of the mother and her children, the male partners coming and going at the woman's choice: an ideal which many feminists might regard as a reversion to a stereotype of woman as essentially maternal and child-bound. A second complication is that, when she does produce children, she is open to the reproaches of Father Time that she has added to the world's misery by bringing more unwilling lives into this vale of sorrows. (Sue has good reason to wish that 'some harmless mode of vegetation might have peopled Paradise'.)[36]

Fourth: Sue, whose happiest phase is that briefly-treated period when she is said to be living in bliss ('Greek joyousness') with Jude outside wedlock, can be seen as a forerunner of those women who, in more permissive times, fulfil themselves sexually without being bound formally to one partner. Against this, however, stands the novel's own ambiguity about the society of the future: perhaps it will be more enlightened and tolerant (Jude and Sue being 'fifty years too soon'), but perhaps it will be worse, for the sensitive may gradually express 'the coming universal wish not to live'; and, in any case, society, it is suggested, must always remain bound to that nature whose law is 'mutual butchery'. A further complication is the ambivalence of treatment of nature itself: it is described not only as a site of torment but also as the basis of joy:

'I said it was Nature's intention . . . . . that we should be joyful in what instincts she afforded us . . . . . And now Fate has given us this stab in the back for being such fools as to take Nature at her word!' [37]

Even the novel's recurrent (and often satirical) criticisms of marriage receive a cogent challenge voiced by Arabella. Her terms may be reductive, but there is an element of practical common sense within her appraisal of entry to wedlock:

'Life with a man is more business-like after it, and money matters work better. And then, you see, if you have rows, and he turns you out of doors, you can get the law to protect you, which you can't otherwise, unless he half runs you through with a knife, or cracks your noddle with a poker. And if he bolts away from you – I say it friendly, as woman to woman, for there's never any knowing what a man med do – you'll have the sticks o' furniture, and won't be looked upon as a thief.' [38]

Against Sue's resistance to marriage as a ground for sexual coercion of the sensitive woman, Arabella here offers a shrewd and sisterly ('woman to woman') reminder that marriage can offer economic and legal security which the female might otherwise lack. Arabella's evident materialism ('you'll have the sticks o' furniture') qualifies her case but does not undermine it.

Sue's resistance to stereotyping, her repeated evasion of the roles that a relative, headmistress, husband or lover would seek to impose on her, does partly serve to question stereotyping in general. Here is a personality struggling to elude the meshes of custom, convention and cliché-bound language. Sue, we are told, 'was beginning to be so puzzling and unpredicable' (later, 'unstateable'). [39] One of Hardy's projects was indeed to challenge the 'predicable' or 'stateable', and that project is qualified but not cancelled by those passages towards the end of the novel, particularly in VI.iii, in which Jude and Sue retrospectively analyse and summarize their respective characters. It is partly countered by the narrator's readiness to generalize about 'narrow womanly humours', the sad lot of 'The Weaker [Sex]', and woman's subjection to 'injustice, loneliness, child-bearing, and bereavement'. [40]

As we have seen, comparison with the New Woman fiction which burgeoned in the period 1893–5 does make some aspects of Sue's character and outlook seem less original and progressive than they might otherwise seem. On the other hand, Sue lives more vividly and convincingly as a creation than do almost all the other New Women of that time. By innumerable touches of detail (even the angle of her thumb), Hardy makes her live in the imagination: vibrant, tremulous, vivacious, vulnerable.

> Sue, in her new summer clothes, flexible and light as a bird, her little thumb stuck up by the stem of her white cotton sunshade, went along as if she hardly touched ground, and as if a moderately strong puff of wind would float her over the hedge into the next field.[41]

Jude the Obscure criticizes people's inhumanity to people; it indicts social injustice, puritanical prejudice and the grip of stereotypes upon the volatility of human life; and thereby the novel aids the feminist cause simply by being a poignantly humane text which advocates greater tolerance and kindly feeling between people. To the extent that it is feministic, it is so only as an aspect of its larger moral project. As Jude says:

> '[I]nstead of protesting against the conditions [some women] protest against the man, the other victim; just as a woman in a crowd will abuse the man who crushes against her, when he is only the helpless transmitter of the pressure put upon him.'

'Yes', comments Sue: 'some are like that, instead of uniting with the man against the common enemy, coercion.'[42]

5.5.2 LITTLE FATHER TIME – AGAIN

As we have seen, the main dispute about the characterization of Little Father Time is whether it should be seen as failure or as a valuable challenge to the realistic mode. Critics who see it as a failure claim generally that the depiction is implausible and that here Hardy's pessimism runs to melodramatic excess; those who see it as a valuable challenge claim that Hardy is voicing discontent with the conservative aspects of realism by offering a subversive disruption.

We have noted various objections to the latter view. First: there is no necessary correlation of realism with conservatism; when the realistic novel first strongly emerged, it was seen as a radical challenge to conventional romantic fiction; and realism could be called a democratic mode rather than a conservative mode, given its continuing widespread popularity in the cinema and in televised drama, as well as in fiction. Second: alternative modes which characterize experimental fiction have no necessary correlation with, say, left-wing views. In addition, it is notable that critics who purport to oppose realism still use, in their own critical essays, the convention of realistic prose discourse: they write in a manner which mimics the educated speaking voice and which gives prominence to rational co-ordination and to empirical evidence.

The presentation of Little Father Time is not the astringently disruptive shock that such critics suggest. From the start of *Jude the Obscure*, Hardy's predominantly realistic mode has been heightened by strong thematic co-ordination and by a compression of effect which often gives the various scenes some symbolic qualities. With Time, however, that tension between realistic depiction and symbolic intent which, hitherto, on the whole, was well reconciled, now becomes marked and strained. As child travelling and as child conversing in frightened tones to Sue, he is reasonably plausible, though his persistent and recalcitrant pessimism strains belief. As depressed, traumatized and frightened child he is credible; as possessor of metaphysical insight into 'Creation's groan', he is incredible. Intermittently, Hardy strains to invest Time's gloom with the wisdom of a quasi-supernatural seer, and at those points the prose becomes speciously rhetorical in its assertiveness:

He was Age masquerading as Juvenility ..... A ground swell from ancient years of night seemed now and then to lift the child in this his morning-life, when his face took a back view over some great Atlantic of time, and appeared not to care about what it saw.[43]

The effect is of an explicit and portentous pessimism imposed by the narrator rather than of a designed clash of literary modes. Clearly intended as a sacrificial victim possessed of intuitively Schopenhauerian wisdom about life's wretchedness, Time seems a schematically exaggerated and compressed vehicle for the bleak outlook implicit in the whole story of Jude and Sue. He appears to personify the misanthropy which various narratorial comments had voiced: for example, the narrator's claim in I.ii that Jude was the sort of person 'who was born to ache a good deal before the fall of the curtain upon his unnecessary life should signify that all was well with him again'. Yet since the reader has, by VI.ii, become familiar with such pessimistic comments, the death of Time seems not, as Widdowson and Wotton have suggested, an unexpected subversion of expectations, but rather an unfortunately crude endorsement of them. Far from a valuably unpredictable challenge to the realistic convention, the effect is of a confirmation of the predictable danger that Hardy might overstate his philosophical pessimism; and such over-emphasis weakens rather than confirms that negativity.

When discussing the works of Graham Greene, Arnold Kettle pointed out that while an easily identifiable form of sentimentality depicts the world as better than it really is, a less easily identifiable form depicts the world as worse than it really is.[44] In the desire to combat the positive mystification by Dickens of the death of children, Hardy has been led to a negative mystification and towards pessimistic sentimentality. Little Jude Fawley is the atheistic terrible twin of the devout Paul Dombey.

5.5.3 STRUCTURE

Whereas Mary Jacobus claimed that 'The death of the children is the most flagrant instance of Hardy's preparedness to sacrifice verisimilitude to his diagrammatic design', Peter Widdowson (repeating the notion of Eagleton and Wotton) argued that the 'diagrammatic design' is in fact 'a formal demystification of the illusory fictions of realism and humanism'.[45] The problem is whether Hardy has indeed regrettably sacrificed realism or valuably demystified it; so this problem of structure is an extension of the problem of the characterization of Little Time.

Reflection reminds us that realism is not a corrupting mystery in need of demystification; readers are not as gullible as the Marxists suggest. In the 1970s and 1980s it was fashionable to argue that readers of 'realist novels' were so credulous that they believed they were looking not at a work of fiction but through a window at the real world. Among the critics adopting this naïve assumption was Terence Hawkes, who said that (thanks to the work of Roland Barthes) we can now see that Balzac, for instance, 'turns out to be no "realist" at all. His narrative affords no transparent "innocent" window on to a "reality" that lies "beyond" the text.'[46] This doctrine underestimated the intelligence of readers, who can distinguish between a novel and a window, who never suppose that they are in danger of being wounded by bullets fired by a revolver in a story, and who know that if a work is fictional it offers a hypothetical and value-laden account of the world. Like Catherine Belsey in her account of Shakespeare's *The Winter's Tale*, [47] however, various Marxist commentators on *Jude the Obscure* assumed that noticeable artifice (whether schematic plotting, frequent citations of literary texts within a work of fiction, or shifts towards symbolism) must valuably 'undermine the illusion'. As Hamlet and the Players remind us, a work which explicitly invokes and discusses fictionality may thereby be strengthening its imaginative force, not subverting it; the discussion may be a sign of self-confidence, not schizophrenia.

Discussions of the techniques of *Jude the Obscure* can usefully be guided by reference to the distinctive features of Hardy's poetry. Consider that poem 'Hap', quoted in Part 3.2. It uses traditional formal devices: the sonnet form, with its taut rhyme-scheme and metre of iambic pentameter. Its diction and syntax vary between the realistically colloquial and the muscularly contorted – the contortions being imposed partly by the needs of the rhyme-scheme. Simple diction alternates with relatively technical, specialized diction ('Crass Casualty', 'purblind Doomsters'). The argument twists and turns economically but with the contortions and muscularity lent by compression and formal constraint. Hardy said that his poetry sought to emulate the 'cunning irregularity' of Gothic architecture. In the structure of his novels, Hardy (the former architect) likes the ironies and the implication of cosmic mockery which are induced by an ingeniously patterned plot, just as in his poetry he likes the ordinances of rhythm and phrasing which are induced by formally patterned constraints. Yet, within that firmly structured plot, he seeks to refer frankly and directly to contemporaneous realities, just as, in his poems, he seeks to employ some simple, direct, colloquial phrases. In short, what Hardy values is the sense of combat between the spontaneous and the formally resistant, between the natural and the architectural, between the vital and its ubiquitous adversaries. His techniques thus imply his world-view.

In *Jude the Obscure*, he clearly values the effect of human struggles against and within the stark entanglements of a coincidence-laden world. To a large extent, his structuring of events is vindicated by the sharp ironies, thematic polemics and vivid human responses which are facilitated by that structuring. Generally, though with some clear exceptions, the effect is not of realism being undermined but of realism being intensified in its moral and philosophical significance. Realism is usually tedious when it merely reports, but vivifying when it is inflected so as to surprise us into fresh appreciation of the real. *Jude the Obscure*, for all its structural symmetries, does not have a plot dictated by human intrigue, villainy or melodramatic machination. In its taut mesh of ironies move characters who are vagrant in the sense that they roam to and fro both geographically and ideologically; they undergo reversals in situation, emotion and belief. Hence, as Mary Jacobus said, this novel seems 'at once fixed and fluid, over-emphatic and true to life': 'Events which seem contrived precipitate inner changes which are painfully authenticated.'[48] Within the contrived trap, characters respond intensely, engagingly, plausibly and pointedly to the conditions of their entrapment. The main weakness, as early reviewers noted, is that Hardy sometimes seems to be exercising the very powers of a cruel deity or cosmic will which he wishes to indict. G. K. Chesterton called him 'a sort of village atheist brooding and blaspheming over the village idiot'.[49] If Hardy sometimes wishes to shake his fist at his Creator, the reader may wish to shake his or her fist at the manipulative creator of *Jude the Obscure*.

Such manipulation, however, is combative. So many novels by other writers had been providential in their plot-patterns. Richardson's Pamela, after her vicissitudes, wins the hand of her wealthy master. Jane Eyre, after all her sufferings, at last inherits a fortune and wins the man she loves. Margaret Hale (in *North and South*) similarly inherits wealth and at last marries her ardent wooer. In these and so many similar cases, divine Providence seems to reward the staunchly pious heroine. In *Jude the Obscure*, therefore, the adversarial Thomas Hardy designed a defiantly and ruthlessly anti-providential structure.

Moral flexibility remains, nevertheless, because of the ambivalence of central characterizations (which attract both sympathy and criticism from the reader) and because the narrator displays variable authority and consistency. Sometimes Sue, for example, appears more intelligent than the narrator. Hardy may thus seem to lack the poise displayed by various other major novelists; he seems partly subject to the divisions which his characters voice and enact. Vicarious self-pity is evident. Consequently, his stance may appear *less authoritative* but *more intimately expressive*.

5.5.4 LANGUAGE

'I love the place – although I know how it hates all men like me – the so-called Self-taught, – how it scorns our laboured acquisitions, when it should be the first to respect them; how it sneers at our false quantities and mispronunciations, when it should say, I see you want help, my poor friend!'[50]

Hardy's language is sometimes uncouth or ponderously pedantic; his characters often orate theatrically instead of conversing naturally; perhaps they and he have the autodidact's fondness for parading learning which is not properly assimilated. Such were the complaints made in many reviews and subsequent critical accounts of the novels.

Some concessions should probably be made to these plaintiffs. Hardy's phrasing can sometimes display the circumlocutions of a pedant, as when Sue blinks away 'an access of eye moisture', or Jude submits to Arabella's 'midnight contiguity', or Arabella introduces Jude to 'the varieties of spirituous delectation'.[51] (Even these phrases could be defended as evidence of a mildly ironic or mock-heroic stance by the narrator.) Occasionally he sounds like a Victorian guidebook, as in the opening of IV.i, which indeed paraphrases a tourists' guide to Shaftesbury. Some of his allusions to lesser-known artists (e.g., Sassoferrato and Sebastiano) may be imposing rather than illuminating. If we consider the characters, Jude's linguistic development from the lad's marked Wessex accent to the young intellectual's fluent middle-class phraseology may seem remarkably rapid; and the dialogue between Jude and Sue frequently modulates into lofty debating-society rhetoric. At this point, however, the concessions to hostile critics may become too generous. Jude chalks on a college wall:

'I have understanding as well as you; I am not inferior to you: yea, who knoweth not such things as these?' – Job xii. 3.[52]

Jude's reproach is also Hardy's.

As Raymond Williams pointed out, those who refer to Thomas Hardy as an 'autodidact' may be using the term snobbishly, to imply that as a person who lacked a university education and was partly self-instructed, Hardy may have failings thought characteristic of the self-taught – particularly a gauche or uncritical way of displaying learning.[53] Certainly, Williams was right to note that Hardy had a longer and fuller formal education than the vast majority of men in the mid-nineteenth century. If the word be used in an unsnobbish sense, 'autodidact' can still be applied to him, however, for he strove to educate himself culturally in his spare time, translating Latin, Greek, French and German, reading intellectual articles in reviews, studying scientific, classical and philosophical works, making numerous and sometimes lengthy notes, and thus preparing a storehouse of ideas for use in the poems and fiction.

Jude, far less successfully than his author, is the autodidact fired by intellectual ambition. He seeks an alternative homeland in the wider cultural world; and he makes great progress, even though he cannot fulfil the ambition to enter Church or University. If he sounds at times pedantic or 'preachy', this is partly to make the authorial point that intellectually he is well suited to the careers which are denied to him. ('Well preached!', says Tinker Taylor, after a particularly eloquent declamation.) Jude's mind becomes so literary that even when he eventually declares '[I]t was my poverty and not my will that consented to be beaten', he is quoting (apparently unconsciously) the words of the Apothecary in *Romeo and Juliet*: 'My poverty, but not my will, consents.'[54]

One obvious irony is that Jude becomes socially and linguistically uprooted as a consequence of his aspirations. This is made plain by the frequent contrasts between his diction and the rural or working-class idioms of Widow Edlin, Aunt Drusilla and the various workmen he encounters: his language marks him out as largely middle-class by culture, even though, as a struggling artisan, he exists on the lowest fringe of the middle class. And, of course, the relatively ungrammatical speech of the working classes can still prove vividly direct and to the point; often reductive, but astutely so. Take the carter's account of Christminster in I.iii, for instance:

'O, they never look at anything that folks like we can understand ..... On'y foreign tongues used before the Flood, when no two families spoke alike. They read that sort of thing as fast as a night-hawk will whir. 'Tis all learning there – nothing but learning, except religion. And that's learning too, for I never could understand it. Yes, 'tis a serious-minded place. Not but there's wenches in the streets o' nights ..... You know, I suppose, that they raise pa'sons there like radishes in a bed? And though it do take – how many years, Bob? – five years to turn a lirruping hobble-de-hoy chap into a solemn preaching man with no corrupt passions, they'll do it, if it can be done, and polish un off like the workmen they be, and turn un out wi' a long face .....'⁵⁵

In this account of the Christminster worlds there is a mixture of ignorance and unwittingly astute satire: this is praise that mocks and, with surprising cogency, summons up a picture of a parson-factory in which black-coated preachers are manufactured like chair-legs by the 'workmen' of this new Tower of Babel whose concerns seem suspiciously remote from everyday life.

Later, when Jude returns briefly to Marygreen after settling in Christminster, a workman (John) remarks that in his own view the so-called 'City of Light' had seemed little more than 'auld crumbling buildings, half church, half almshouse, and not much going on at that'; and the following conversation ensues:

'You are wrong, John; there is more going on than meets the eye of a man walking through the streets. It is a unique centre of thought and religion – the intellectual and spiritual granary of this country. All that silence and absence of goings-on is the stillness of infinite motion – the sleep of the spinning-top, to borrow the simile of a writer.'

'O, well, it med be all that, or it med not. As I say, I didn't see nothing of it the hour or two I was there; so I went in and had a pot o' beer, and a penny loaf, and a ha'porth o' cheese, and waited till it was time to come along home. You've j'ined a College by this time, I suppose?'

'Ah, no!' said Jude. 'I am almost as far off that as ever.'

'How so?'

Jude slapped his pocket.

'Just what we thought! Such places be not for such as you – only for them with plenty o' money.'⁵⁶

The balance in this dialogue is finely calculated. Against Jude's idealistic intellectual diction, with its quotation from William Davenant, moves the blunt colloquial strength of working-class idiom and a common sense which, in the event, is vindicated by Jude's failure to enter the university. The appeal of such parts of *Jude the Obscure* is mixed: the exchange wins the reader's sympathy not only because of its literary strengths but also because the reader recognizes that Hardy is here helping that movement which would eventually make university entry in Britain somewhat less exclusive and more democratic.

Again, if Jude and Sue sometimes speak pedantically or over-intellectually, Hardy is usually aware of this and shows himself shrewdly eager for a challenging contrast. Arabella's blunt talking can disconcert Sue and comically offset Jude; and even Phillotson can colloquially challenge a learned citation of J. S. Mill by Sue ('What do I care about J. S. Mill . . . . . I only want to lead a quiet life!').⁵⁷ Again, when Drusilla is dying, Widow Edlin sends a telegram with the news, 'Your aunt is sinking. Come at once'; and, in contrast to this telegraphic curtness and the cliché ('is sinking'), Hardy deploys the labourer who tells Jude, 'She wouldn't have knowed 'ee. She lay like a doll wi' glass eyes . . . . .'⁵⁸ Here the labourer's image of the 'doll wi' glass eyes' gives a starker reality to the dying Drusilla than more 'educated' diction might have done.

In such ways, *Jude the Obscure* gains a distinctive linguistic texture, rich and intelligently varied. It has deliberate 'polyphonic' qualities: a systematic critical deployment of contrasting language-conventions. In his poems and his prose, Hardy loved the mixture of textures created by different linguistic traditions. He relished Dorset dialect; but, as one who had studied classical languages long and hard, he also relished the way in which a knowledge of Latin gives magical precision to so many lengthy latinate English words; and he could not resist a Greek jest in the name 'Tetuphenay' ('Beater').⁵⁹ If the dialogue of Jude and Sue sometimes seems stiltedly literary, it is not unlike the real-life dialogue of some earnest young intellectuals in the past; and a poignant quality of the text is notable in the intermittent collusion between the style of the studious Jude and the style of the learned narrator. As Hardy's poems effect distinctive juxtapositions of abstract, concrete, colloquial and latinate, rustic and urbane, familiar and oddly technical, so Hardy's novel aims at an extensive polyphony which is also an extensive system of valuation. The style of *Jude the Obscure* is full of friction, contrasts, collisions and ironic allusions; and it is thus highly appropriate to the cultural flux and ideological confusion which is its subject.

Through speech-idioms, Hardy notes the gains and the losses resulting from the achievement of a 'cultivated' mode of discourse. Again, he offers an abundance of quotations and literary citations for a diversity of ironic purposes. The Bible which Jude studies both inspires and mocks him: he becomes a second Job without Job's salvation; a Moses who never reaches the promised land; a Paul among jeering disciples. The texts studied by Jude sometimes warn him ineffectually of the snares of the senses, and sometimes celebrate the erotic. Sue points out the ways in which even the sacred texts have been falsified hypocritically, the sensuous verses of the 'Song of Solomon' having been cloaked by the bowdlerizing allegoric commentary of the translators. Mill and von Humboldt provide intellectual support for Sue in her demand for freedom from Phillotson; they also offer a vision of existence which can hardly be realized in nineteenth-century conditions. Sometimes a romantic text can nourish a narcissistic vanity, as when Sue basks in the romanticism of Shelley's 'Epipsychidion':

> A seraph of Heaven, too gentle to be human,
> Veiling beneath that radiant form of woman ...

Typically of this novel, the romantic text both aids idealistic aspiration and is mocked by the mundane realities in which Jude and Sue struggle. As Don Quixote was an anachronism, fired by the spirit of antiquated literary chivalry while living in a mediocre world, so Jude can be seen as quixotic not only in his attempt to live by the light of the ancient and sacred texts which he so laboriously studies, but also in the learning which enables him to recite the Greek Athanasian creed in a tavern to a largely uncomprehending audience. The cruel clash of text with reality is repeatedly emphasized. Jude and Sue seek to earn their living by restoring the Ten Commandments painted in a church, but both are discharged when it is discovered that they are breaking the commandment 'Thou shalt not commit adultery'. When Jude's children are found dead, the background music is the organ of the college chapel playing the anthem from the seventy-third Psalm, 'Truly God is loving unto Israel'. And when the drunken Jude is half-carried by Arabella to her bedroom, the text he ludicrously cites is 'Though I give my body to be burned, and have not charity, it profiteth me nothing.' Again and again these biblical and literary citations, by their lofty tone and resonant significances, offset and ironically accentuate the baseness of so much mundane experience; yet, intermittently, the mundane experiences challenge the authority and validity of the cited texts. Even the formal language of legal officialdom seems to mock – and is mocked by – Jude and Sue:

'Names and Surnames of Parties' – (they were to be parties now, not lovers, she thought). 'Condition' – (a horrid idea) – 'Rank or Occupation' – 'Age' – 'Dwelling at' – 'Length of Residence' – 'Church or Building in which the Marriage is to be solemnized' – 'District and County in which the Parties respectively dwell.'

'It spoils the sentiment, doesn't it!' she said on their way home.[60]

This polyphony of different idioms, languages, class dialects, literary styles and modes, biblical and classical texts, folk idioms, vulgar slang and legal jargon gives a distinctive texture of cultural exploration and social questioning to *Jude the Obscure*. Hardy voices a volatile mixture of styles, values, assumptions and ethical conflicts. One of the most proleptic features of the novel is, of course, its readiness to suggest ways in which modes of discourse may shape, mould, facilitate or repress the varying lives of human beings. The twentieth-century dramatist Eugène Ionesco noted in his diary:

Words have killed images, or are concealing them. A civilization of words is a civilization lost.

In stark contrast, the philosopher A. J. Ayer wrote:

Neurath's comment on the famous last sentence of the *Tractatus* 'Whereof one cannot speak, thereof one must be silent' was that 'One must indeed be silent, but not about anything' and Ramsey pointed out, in another context, that 'What you can't say, you can't say and you can't whistle it either.'[61]

It is an indication of the dialectical richness of *Jude the Obscure* that both these contrasting views are clearly suggested by its text.

Arabella deserves the last word here. When Jude is exhausted and embittered, he declares: 'I've finished myself – put an end to a feverish life which ought never to have been begun!' And Arabella replies: 'Lord – you do talk lofty! Won't you have something warm to drink?'[62]

117

Part 6 Conclusion: How the Text Criticizes Its Critics

Jude the Obscure moves through time, changing and veering as language and society evolve. Frequently, critics who value it highly seek (egoistically) to suggest that the text astutely endorses their own prejudices; hostile critics, in contrast, seek to blame the text for its failure to endorse their own prejudices. Time has eroded some of this novel's force and blunted some of its sharp teeth, so that to recognize its original vigour we need to exercise the historical imagination; yet it has largely retained its cogency, since the problems it presents are still with us – problems concerning social justice, equality of opportunity, social mobility, the reconciliation of sexual needs with social order, the reconciliation of the often conflicting claims of male and female, and the reconciliation of individual liberty with familial and social responsibility.

Jude the Obscure soon put to shame the narrow-minded early reviewers who deemed it immoral and degrading. It is now those reviewers who seem immoral in their reluctance to appreciate the novel's humanity. *Jude the Obscure* was, in its time, courageous in its onslaught on religious dogmatism and on sentimental providentialism; courageous, too, in its frank presentation of sexual entanglements and confusions. Even today, it has dated markedly less than many other novels of its age; and its durability derives largely from Hardy's iconoclastic, questing intelligence. That intelligence manifests itself most forcefully in his ironic complexity, a readiness not only to test pious and respectable orthodoxies against the familiar if unpalatable facts of life, and to stage ironic contrasts between the two, but also to dramatize mutually heightening, mutually questioning contrasts: contrasts between the enhancive and the reductive, the sacred and the profane, the abstract and the concrete, the intellectual and the instinctive. Again, he could press into exposure the tensions and ambiguities which lurked within familiar concepts: were the instincts to be seen as the natural ground of being, falsified by civilization, or as the turbulent grossness which civilization strives to control and refine? Was sexuality to be allowed freer fulfilment or to be regarded as nature's cruellest snare? Did education exalt or deracinate the individual? Was questing social ambition a sign of idealism or of the modern malaise of restlessness? Was thought itself a boon or 'a disease of flesh'?

We have noted the novel's faults, among them the confusions, the over-insistent pessimism and the 'negative sentimentality'; but when we consider its range of topics and their vigour of presentation, *Jude the Obscure* seems a remarkably adroit, compressed work. Though it reflects so many Victorian debates (about religion and its decline, about science and evolution, about class and education), the intelligent verve of its challenges to various orthodoxies makes it a forerunner of the future, anticipating the scepticism and iconoclasm of the twentieth century. Even now, *Jude the Obscure* retains a quality of challenging unfamiliarity because of its refusal to submit tamely to conventional literary-critical criteria or to more recent theories of the novel. It stubbornly denies Flaubertian detachment, Jamesian urbanity, Proustian sophistication or the introspections of the 'stream of consciousness'. Its spleen and anger defy critics who speak of 'the death of the author': this is the most outspoken work of the very distinctive Thomas Hardy. In outline it may seem almost too schematic; but its complexity, fluidity and paradoxicality in themes and characterization resist the paraphrasing commentator. Yet this complexity is not achieved at the price of emotional force. It remains a painful, almost harrowing book to read, as can be well recognized by students (since an ardent but frustrated student is a central character), or by lovers (since two well-meaning lovers come to wretchedness), or by striving women (since a striving woman is beaten down), or by married couples (since its questioning of marriage remains cogent). Yet its painfulness is mitigated by the elements of satire, farce, burlesque, deft irony and linguistic relish.

Critical accounts of the novel are trapped in the discourse of rational expository prose: in such accounts, the abstract, the theoretical, the logical and the linear predominate. In his novel, however, Hardy could mix, blend and contrast the abstract and the concrete, the intellectual and the emotional, the didactic and the comic, the expository and the satiric. He builds irony upon irony. Consequently, *Jude the Obscure* will always outdistance its commentators, for they can attempt elucidation but can never offer equivalents to its effects. The novel works partly through arguments but largely through images, scenes, patterns and imaginary people: all of them can shift and vary in the memory, combining now in one structure of possible significance and now in another. Recent critics have said much of 'ideology', of 'discourse', of 'bourgeois humanism'; they seem reluctant to talk of truth, liberty, love and happiness. Yet *Jude the Obscure* is one of the most moving of novels in the energy of its struggle to dramatize the quest for those very objects: truth, liberty, love and happiness. It can still make the eyes prickle with sympathy, still evoke a grin at human folly, and still elicit anger against modes of oppression. While searching realities, it offers us also an imaginative interlude from the immediate pressure of realities. We read for imaginative pleasure, not for didactic instruction; though, if the pleasure be intelligent, the instruction comes as a by-product, and then not as a simple imparting of information so much as from the varied provocations to fresh thought and feeling.

One familiar but partly evasive way of dealing with *Jude the Obscure* is to seek to paraphrase it politically and then judge it according to whether we agree or disagree with the politics we have thereby elicited. This way has its uses but can be reductive; it is also, in one respect, arbitrary. Politics (like every area of ethical discourse) defies logic, in the sense that from logical premises which are factual, one cannot consistently derive a conclusion which is a political value-judgement: there is always a logical void between 'is' and 'ought to be'. Whatever its paraphrasable doctrinal tenor, a major novel like *Jude the Obscure* is humanly rewarding because of its apparently non-doctrinal character-istics of articulate intelligence, imagination and sensitivity. The history of literary criticism itself suggests this. One admirable critic, Samuel Johnson, was a Tory Anglican; another, Jean-Paul Sartre, was an atheis-tic Marxist. This shows that the merit of a critic depends not on his or her doctrinal assumptions (however much they may pervade the writing) but on the intelligence of his or her responsiveness to the works under discussion. Principles, prejudices and procedures can readily be imparted by instruction; acumen cannot. And the acumen of Thomas Hardy's *Jude the Obscure* is implicit in the totality of its articulately imaginative responsiveness to life.

What? – 'the totality of its articulately imaginative responsiveness to life'? You know what would happen in the novel to someone talking like that: the speaker would be struck on the ear by a pig's pizzle, or be greeted by a sardonic 'Well preached!' or an admonitory 'Keep yer tongue quiet, my man, while the procession passes.' And that makes my point. *Jude the Obscure* will continue to be read, to provoke emotions and arguments, and to extend our beleaguered selves, when most of its commentators have sunk into oblivion.

Part 7 Caudal

7.1 Notes

Unless otherwise indicated, all quotations from *Jude the Obscure* are from the first edition, published in London by Osgood, McIlvaine & Co. in 1895. For purposes of comparison and ease of reference, I have added in brackets the page number of the corresponding passage in the current Penguin edition, by C. H. Sisson (London: Penguin, 1985). The attentive reader will see various differences between some of the quoted passages and their Penguin versions.

PART 2 (pp. 3–21)

1. F. E. Hardy: *The Later Years of Thomas Hardy* (London: Macmillan, 1930), p. 196.
2. W. B. Yeats: *Mythologies* (London: Macmillan, 1959), p. 331.
3. Letter of 1927 cited in Michael Millgate: *Thomas Hardy: A Biography* (Oxford: Oxford University Press, 1982), p. 26.
4. *Later Years*, p. 176.
5. *Later Years*, p. 260; *Jude* (1895), p. 20 (Penguin, p. 61).
6. Samuel Johnson: *Rasselas* (London: Oxford University Press, 1887), p. 67.
7. J.-H. Bernardin de Saint-Pierre: *Paul and Virginia*; Sophie Cottin: *Elizabeth; or, The Exiles of Siberia* (London: Noble, 1850), pp. 74–5.
8. *Jude*, p. 290 (Penguin, p. 295, corrects 'Cynthia' to 'Cythna').
9. *Jude*, pp. 6–7 (Penguin, p. 50).
10. *The Collected Letters of Thomas Hardy*, Vol. I, ed. R. L. Purdy and M. Millgate (Oxford: Oxford University Press, 1978), p. 7.
11. Millgate: *Thomas Hardy*, pp. 7–8, and photograph facing p. 144.
12. Millgate: *Thomas Hardy*, pp. 133, 164.
13. F. E. Hardy: *The Early Life of Thomas Hardy* (London: Macmillan, 1928), p. 81.
14. Millgate: *Thomas Hardy*, p. 130.
15. This paragraph cites reviews reprinted in *Thomas Hardy: The Critical Heritage*, ed. R. G. Cox (London: Routledge & Kegan Paul, 1970), pp. 1–8.
16. *Early Life*, p. 116.
17. *A Supplement to the Oxford English Dictionary* (Oxford: Clarendon Press, 1986), p. 1257, cites Barnes's *Poems of Rural Life* (1868) as the earliest usage

of 'Wessex' for the region in modern times, followed by Hardy in *Cornhill Magazine* (November 1874, p. 624).

18. *Early Life*, pp. 116–17; Millgate: *Thomas Hardy*, pp. 141–2; *Thomas Hardy: The Critical Heritage*, pp. xv–xvi.

19. *A Pair of Blue Eyes* (London: Penguin, 1986), pp. 271–2.

20. *Thomas Hardy: The Critical Heritage*, p. xvi.

21. Simon Gatrell: *Hardy the Creator* (Oxford: Oxford University Press, 1988), p. 228; A. L. Bowley: *Wages and Income in the United Kingdom since 1860* (London: Cambridge University Press, 1937), p. 49.

22. *Collected Letters*, I, p. 28.

23. Gatrell, p. 228.

24. *Early Life*, p. 192.

25. *Critical Heritage*, pp. xxxvii–xxxviii.

26. *Critical Heritage*, pp. xxxi–xxxii; Gatrell, pp. 251–3 and 241.

27. *Early Life*, p. 262.

28. 'Postscript' (1912) to *Jude* (Penguin), p. 40; *Critical Heritage*, p. xxxvi.

29. *Critical Heritage*, pp. xxxiii–xxxiv, 291–9, 284–91, 256–62.

30. *Later Years*, p. 65.

31. *Later Years*, p. 58.

32. *Critical Heritage*, p. xxviii; Gatrell, pp. 252, 238.

33. *Critical Heritage*, p. 371.

34. Donald Davie: *Thomas Hardy and British Poetry* (London: Routledge & Kegan Paul, 1973), p. 3.

35. Chapter 3 of Peter Widdowson's *Hardy in History* (London and New York: Routledge, 1989) has a useful discussion of Hardy's works on radio, film and television.

36. Marcel Proust: *A la recherche du temps perdu*, XII: *La Prisonnière* [II] (Paris: Gallimard, 1949), pp. 217, 218. (Proust notes 'cette géométrie du tailleur de pierre dans les romans de Thomas Hardy' and 'tous ces romans superposables les uns aux autres, comme les maisons verticalement entassées en hauteur sur le sol pierreux de l'île'.) F. E. Hardy: *Later Years*, pp. 59, 248.

37. D. H. Lawrence: *Study of Thomas Hardy* in *Phoenix* [Vol. I] (London: Heinemann, 1936); John Fowles: 'Hardy and the Hag' in Lance St John Butler: *Thomas Hardy after Fifty Years* (London: Macmillan, 1977), pp. 28–42.

38. Mrs Emma Hardy was reported to have said that if she had read the manuscript of *Jude*, 'it would *not* have been published, or at least, not without considerable emendation'. (Millgate: *Thomas Hardy*, p. 380.)

39. *Jude*, p. 15 (Penguin, p. 57). Cf.: '[H]e came to the conclusion that he did not wish to grow up' (*Early Life*, p. 19).

40. Carl J. Weber: *Hardy of Wessex* (London: Routledge & Kegan Paul, 1965), pp. 10–11, 23–4, 41–2, 63, 76, 199–206.

41. Weber, p. 202; *Jude*, p. 220 (Penguin, p. 234).

42. *Jude*, p. v (Penguin, p. 39).

43. *Jude* (Penguin), p. 39. Although, in reprints, these words now form part of the 'Preface to the First Edition' which bears the date 1895, the actual preface to the first London edition did *not* include them. Here Hardy rewrote history.

PART 3 (pp. 22–51)

1. *The Letters of Henry James*, Vol. I, ed. Percy Lubbock (London: Macmillan, 1920), p. 194; *Henry James: Letters*, Vol. III, ed. Leon Edel (London: Macmillan, 1981), pp. 406–7.
2. See 'Janiform Novels' in Cedric Watts: *The Deceptive Text* (Brighton: Harvester, 1984), pp. 13–29.
3. *Jude*, p. 10 (Penguin, with variants, p. 53).
4. *In Memoriam*, sections 55–6, in *Tennyson's Poetry*, ed. R. W. Hill, Jr. (New York: Norton, 1971), pp. 147–8.
5. *Joseph Conrad's Letters to R. B. Cunninghame Graham*, ed. Cedric Watts (London: Cambridge University Press, 1969), p. 70.
6. Charles Darwin: *The Origin of Species* (Harmondsworth: Penguin, 1968), pp. 459–60.
7. *Early Life*, p. 198.
8. *Jude*, p. 386 (Penguin, p. 378).
9. *Jude*, p. 13 (Penguin, pp. 55–6).
10. *Jude*, p. 336 (Penguin, p. 333). Later, Gillingham tells Phillotson: 'I was always against your opening the cage-door and letting the bird go' (p. 461; Penguin, pp. 442–3). See also: *Later Years*, pp. 106–7.
11. For Hardy's sceptical note on Saint-Simon, and for his study of Comte, see *The Literary Notebooks of Thomas Hardy*, Vol. I, ed. Lennart A. Björk (London: Macmillan, 1985), pp. xxviii, 311–12. (Harrison is quoted on p. 312.) Comte is cited in Hardy's 'Apology' to *Late Lyrics* (*Complete Poems*, p. 562). Positivists at the Artizans' Society: *Jude*, p. 382 (Penguin, p. 374).
12. 'General Preface' (1911): *Jude* (Penguin), p. 498. Hardy discusses his 'evolutionary meliorism' in *Complete Poems*, pp. 557–8.
13. *Jude*, pp. 505, 504 (Penguin, pp. 482, 480).
14. Hardy owned Schopenhauer's *Two Essays* (London: Bell, 1889) and included Schopenhauer in a list of philosophers 'who have my respect'. See *Literary Notebooks*, I, p. 374. A reviewer of *Jude* scornfully attributed to it the notion that 'baby Schopenhauers are . . . . . coming into the world in shoals' (*Critical Heritage*, p. xxxiii).
15. Arthur Schopenhauer: *Essays and Aphorisms*, tr. R. J. Hollingdale (Harmondsworth: Penguin, 1970), pp. 47–8.
16. *Jude*, p. 424 (Penguin, pp. 410–11).
17. *Jude*, p. 13 (Penguin, p. 56).
18. *Jude* (Penguin), p. 39. (The original 1895 text actually lacks the latter phrase.)

19. *Jude*, p. 427 (Penguin, p. 413).

20. *Jude*, p. 400 (Penguin, p. 389).

21. *Later Years*, p. 176.

22. 'General Preface' (1911): *Jude* (Penguin), p. 497.

23. *Later Years*, pp. 57–8.

24. *Tess of the d'Urbervilles* (London: Penguin, 1985), p. 489; *Later Years*, p. 4.

25. *The Complete Poems of Thomas Hardy*, ed. James Gibson (London: Macmillan, 1976), p. 9.

26. *Later Years*, pp. 217, 217, 218.

27. *Early Life*, p. 282.

28. Bertrand Russell: *Philosophical Essays* (London: Longmans, Green, 1910), p. 70.

29. *Jude*, p. 431 (Penguin, p. 417).

30. 'Preface' (1892) to *Tess of the d'Urbervilles* (London: Penguin, 1985), p. 39; 'Preface' (1895) to *The Return of the Native* (London: Penguin, 1985), p. 49.

31. *The Return of the Native*, p. 315 ('high Promethean fashion'); p. 265 ('cruel satires'); p. 421 ('such tortures'); p. 405 ('sport for Heaven').

32. *Jude*, p. 431 (Penguin, p. 417).

33. *Later Years*, p. 166.

34. *The Dynasts* (London: Macmillan, 1965), p. 525.

35. *Later Years*, p. 125 (and also p. 275).

36. Arthur Schopenhauer: *Two Essays* (London: Bell, 1889), p. 331; see also *Literary Notebooks*, Vol. I, p. 374, and *Later Years*, p. 34.

37. Fyodor Dostoyevsky: *White Nights and Other Stories*, tr. Constance Garnett (London: Heinemann, 1918), p. 73; T. H. Huxley: *Collected Essays*, Vol. I (London: Macmillan, 1894), p. 244; Joseph Conrad: *Nostromo* (London: Harper, 1904), p. 423.

38. *Early Life*, pp. 197.

39. *The Return of the Native*, pp. 110–11, 348.

40. *Later Years*, p. 125.

41. See, for example, 'The Sleep-Worker', 'New Year's Eve' and 'God's Education': *Complete Poems*, pp. 121–2, 277–8, 278–9.

42. *Early Life*, p. 293.

43. *Later Years*, pp. 265–6.

44. *Later Years*, p. 91.

45. *Tess of the d'Urbervilles*, p. 174.

46. *Jude*, pp. 187–8 (Penguin, pp. 206–7).

47. 'Apology' to *Late Lyrics* in *Complete Poems*, p. 561.

48. *In Memoriam*, section 96, 11–12.

49. *Jude*, p. 185 (Penguin, pp. 204–5).

50. Mark XV: 34.

51. Matthew Arnold: *Culture and Anarchy* (London: Cambridge University Press, 1960), p. 132.

52. *Culture and Anarchy*, pp. 54ff., 158.

53. *Culture and Anarchy*, pp. 203–4.

54. J. S. Mill: *On Liberty / Representative Government / The Subjection of Women / Three Essays* (London: Oxford University Press, 1912), pp. 61–2.

55. *On Liberty*, p. 73; *Jude*, p. 280 (Penguin, p. 286).

56. Swinburne: *Poems* (Harmondsworth: Penguin, 1961), pp. 42–3.

57. Swinburne: *Poems*, p. 99.

58. Hardy made extensive notes on Pater's *Marius the Epicurean*: see *Literary Notebooks*, Vol. I, pp. 205–7. He met Pater socially in the 1880s: *Early Life*, pp. 236, 275, 278.

59. *Jude*, p. 95 (Penguin, pp. 126–7).

60. *Later Years*, p. 39.

61. *Jude*, p. 129 (Penguin, p. 156).

62. Matthew Arnold: 'Heine' in *Essays Literary and Critical* (London: Dent, n.d.), p. 104; *Jude*, p. 185 (Penguin, p. 204).

63. *Jude*, p. 257 (Penguin, p. 266); *Later Years*, p. 23. On Fourier and Hardy, see *Literary Notebooks*, Vol. I, p. 240.

64. *The Works of Oscar Wilde* (London: Spring Books, 1963), pp. 936, 924.

65. *Jude* (Penguin), p. 42.

66. J. S. Mill: *On Liberty* . . . . . , pp. 427, 451, 494.

67. Gail Cunningham: *The New Woman and the Victorian Novel* (London: Macmillan, 1978), p. 4. This paragraph and the next use Cunningham's book and Rosemarie Morgan's *Women and Sexuality in the Novels of Thomas Hardy* (London and New York: Routledge, 1988).

68. William Blake: 'London' in *Poetry and Prose of William Blake*, ed. G. Keynes (London: Nonesuch, 1956), p. 75.

69. Charlotte Brontë: *Jane Eyre* (Harmondsworth: Penguin, 1966), p. 141.

70. *Jude*, pp. 322–3 (Penguin, p. 322). Jude is heavily indebted by the law-costs, however. (*Jude*, p. 375; Penguin, p. 368.)

71. *Jude*, p. 486 (Penguin, p. 464, gives 'genuine' for 'ordinary': a satiric improvement by Hardy).

72. *The New Woman and the Victorian Novel*, p. 106.

73. George Egerton: *Keynotes* (London: Mathews and Lane, 1893), pp. 28–9. Hardy read and noted this book while writing *Jude*, and George Egerton praised the characterization of Sue. (Millgate: *Thomas Hardy*, pp. 356–7, 375.)

74. Mona Caird: *Daughters of Danaus* (London: Bliss, Sands & Foster, 1894), p. 226.

75. Phillip Mallett: 'Woman and Marriage in Victorian Society' in *Marriage and Property*, ed. E. M. Craik (Aberdeen: Aberdeen University Press, 1984), p. 182.

76. George Bernard Shaw: 'Preface' to *Plays Unpleasant* (Harmondsworth: Penguin, 1946), p. 14; *Critical Heritage*, p. 278.

77. Ibsen in *A Doll's House*, Shaw in *Mrs Warren's Profession*, for instance.

78. *Later Years*, p. 52; *Jude*, p. 208 (Penguin, p. 223).

79. *Jude*, p. vi (Penguin, p. 39); Penguin, pp. 41–2.

80. *Classical Literary Criticism*, tr. T. S. Dorsch (Harmondsworth: Penguin, 1965), pp. 43–4.

81. Plato: *The Republic*, tr. H. D. P. Lee (Harmondsworth: Penguin, 1955), pp. 379–84. *Classical Literary Criticism*, p. 39.

82. *Jude*, p. 355 (Penguin, p. 350).

83. *Later Years*, p. 40.

84. *Jude*, pp. 107–8 (Penguin, p. 137).

85. *The Letters of D. H. Lawrence*, Vol. I, ed. James T. Boulton (Cambridge: Cambridge University Press, 1979), p. 459.

86. Joseph Conrad: *The Secret Agent* (Harmondsworth: Penguin, 1963), p. 212.

87. *Critical Heritage*, p. 271.

88. *Tess of the d'Urbervilles*, p. 180; *Jude*, p. 412 (Penguin, p. 399).

89. *The Return of the Native*, p. 194.

90. *Critical Heritage*, p. 293.

91. *Later Years*, p. 42.

92. *Critical Heritage*, pp. 266, 268.

PART 4 (pp. 52–89)

1. *Early Life*, p. 273.

2. Millgate: *Thomas Hardy*, pp. 349–50.

3. The London text was identical, even in the American spellings, to the New York text.

4. Norman Page: 'Preface' to *Jude the Obscure* (New York: Norton, 1978).

5. This paragraph is based on my reading of Sussex University's volumes of *Harper's New Monthly Magazine*.

6. Gatrell, pp. 157–64.

7. *Jude*, p. 44 (contrast Penguin, pp. 82–3); Robert C. Slack: 'Hardy's Revisions' in *Jude the Obscure* (New York: Norton, 1978), pp. 333–4.

8. *Jude*, p. 42 (contrast Penguin, p. 81); Slack, p. 332.

9. Slack, pp. 336–8.

10. Cedric Watts: *Joseph Conrad: A Literary Life* (London: Macmillan, 1989), p. 114.

11. *Jude* (Penguin), pp. 495–6.

12. *Later Years*, p. 49.

13. *Jude*, p. vi (Penguin, p. 39).

14. *Later Years*, p. 42.

15. *Later Years*, pp. 43, 40.

16. 'Vicarious self-pity' occurs when an author who appears to be depicting sympathetically some suffering individual, group or class, modifies the depiction and its context so that the sufferer resembles a partly idealized and more pitiable version of (or symbolic counterpart to) the author. The process of modification may be partly unconscious.

17. *Jude*, pp. 362, 366 (Penguin, pp. 357, 360–61).

18. Plato: *The Symposium*, tr. W. Hamilton (Harmondsworth: Penguin, 1951),

p. 64; J.-H. Bernardin de Saint-Pierre: *Paul and Virginia* (London: Noble, 1850), p. 12.

19. *Jude*, p. 372 (Penguin, p. 365).
20. *Jude*, p. 10 (Penguin, p. 53).
21. *Jude*, pp. 356, 486 (Penguin, pp. 351, 464).
22. 'Postscript' (1912) to the preface to *Jude* (Penguin), p. 42.
23. *Later Years*, p. 39.
24. Irving Howe: *Thomas Hardy* (London: Macmillan, 1985), p. 140.
25. Joseph Conrad: *A Personal Record* (London: Dent, 1946), p. 124.
26. Roland Barthes: *Image / Music / Text* (New York: Hill and Wang, 1977), pp. 142–8.
27. Job XLII: 12.
28. *Jude*, p. 7 (Penguin, p. 50).
29. *Jude*, p. 207 (Penguin, p. 222).
30. In 1891 Hardy studied the first edition of *The Golden Bough*. (Millgate: *Thomas Hardy*, p. 315.)
31. Millgate: *Thomas Hardy*, p. 139.
32. *Jude*, pp. 41, 159, 152, 416 (Penguin, pp. 80, 182, 175, 402).
33. *Jude*, p. 72 (Penguin, p. 107).
34. *Jude*, p. 272 (Penguin, p. 279).
35. *Jude*, p. 242 (Penguin, p. 251).
36. *Jude*, p. 400 (Penguin, p. 389).
37. *Jude*, pp. 299, 300 (Penguin, pp. 294, 303).
38. *Jude*, p. 427 (Penguin, p. 413).
39. Schopenhauer: *Essays and Aphorisms*, tr. R. J. Hollingdale (Harmondsworth: Penguin, 1970), pp. 47–8.
40. *Jude*, pp. 52, 83, 477 (Penguin, pp. 89, 117, 457).
41. 'Apology' for *Late Lyrics* in *Complete Poems*, p. 557.
42. *Early Life*, p. 268.
43. *Jude*, p. 504 (Penguin, p. 480).
44. *Jude* (Penguin), p. 42.
45. Cleanth Brooks: *Modern Poetry and the Tradition* (Chapel Hill: University of North Carolina Press, 1939), p. 167.
46. *Jude*, p. 208 (Penguin, p. 223).
47. *Later Years*, p. 42.
48. *Jude*, p. 280, reads 'unpredicable' (i.e. 'indefinable'); Hardy later changed this to 'unstateable' (Penguin, p. 286).
49. Oscar Mandel: *A Definition of Tragedy* (New York: New York University Press, 1961), p. 104.
50. Mandel, p. 20.
51. Morris Weitz: *Hamlet and the Philosophy of Literary Criticism* (London: Faber & Faber, 1965), pp. 309–10.
52. *Jude*, p. 257 (Penguin, p. 265).
53. *Jude*, p. 482 (Penguin, p. 461).
54. Thomas Gray: 'Elegy Written in a Country Churchyard', lines 51–2. Hardy

knew the poem well (hence the title *Far from the Madding Crowd*), and it epitomizes various themes of *Jude the Obscure*.

55. Michael Millgate: *Thomas Hardy: His Career as a Novelist* (London: Bodley Head, 1971), p. 327 (my capitalization).
56. *Jude*, p. 400 (Penguin, p. 389).
57. *Jude*, p. 75. Penguin, p. 110, adds Arabella's 'Hold up the pail to catch the blood, and don't talk!'
58. *Jude*, p. 338 (Penguin, p. 336).
59. *Jude*, pp. 5, 123 (Penguin, pp. 49, 150).
60. *Jude*, p. 462 (Penguin, p. 443).
61. *Poetry and Prose of William Blake*, ed. G. Keynes (London: Nonesuch, 1956), pp. 183, 184, 74.
62. *Early Life*, p. 288.
63. *Jude*, pp. 361, 502 (Penguin, pp. 355, 479).
64. *The Return of the Native*, pp. 194, 195.
65. J. I. M. Stewart: *Thomas Hardy: A Critical Biography* (London: Longman, 1971), p. 189.
66. A. Alvarez: essay appended to *Jude the Obscure*, ed. Norman Page (New York: Norton, 1978); quotation from p. 422.
67. *Jude*, p. 373 (Penguin, p. 366).
68. *Jude*, pp. 422–3 (Penguin, p. 409).
69. Charles Dickens: *Dombey and Son* (London and Glasgow: Collins, 1954), pp. 107, 231.

PART 5 (pp. 90–117)

1. The following citations of contemporaneous reviews are taken from *Thomas Hardy: The Critical Heritage*, ed. R. G. Cox (London: Routledge & Kegan Paul, 1970), pp. xxxii–xxxvi, 249–315.
2. *The Letters of Henry James*, Vol. I, ed. Percy Lubbock (London: Macmillan, 1920), p. 194.
3. T. S. Eliot: *After Strange Gods: A Primer of Modern Heresy* (New York: Harcourt, Brace & Co. [1934]), p. 59.
4. F. R. Leavis: *The Great Tradition* [1948] (Harmondsworth: Penguin, 1962), pp. 33, 140.
5. D. H. Lawrence: *Phoenix* [I] (London: Heinemann, 1936), p. 488.
6. *Phoenix*, p. 496.
7. *Phoenix*, p. 509.
8. Cultural primitivism occurs when a writer commends as desirable a state of being which is far simpler than that of the writer or his assumed readers. 'Soft' primitivism extols a life of hedonistic ease; 'hard' primitivism extols as virtuous an austere life of toil. See A. O. Lovejoy and G. Boas: *Primitivism and Related Ideas in Antiquity* (New York: Octagon Books, 1973), pp. 7–11.
9. *Jude*, pp. 419, 100, 141, 142 (Penguin, pp. 406, 131, 166, 166).

10. Terry Eagleton: *Criticism and Ideology* (London: Verso, 1978), p. 131.
11. Eagleton, p. 131.
12. George Wotton: *Thomas Hardy: Towards a Materialist Criticism* (Goldenbridge: Gill and Macmillan, 1985), p. 84.
13. Wotton, p. 88.
14. Wotton, p. 211.
15. *Jude*, p. 393 (Penguin, p. 383).
16. Peter Widdowson: *Hardy in History: A Study in Literary Sociology* (London and New York: Routledge, 1989), p. 150.
17. Widdowson, p. 218.
18. Widdowson, pp. 223–4.
19. *Jude*, p. 344 (Penguin, p. 341).
20. Kate Millett: *Sexual Politics* (London: Virago Press, 1977), pp. 133–4.
21. Mary Jacobus: 'Sue the Obscure' in *Essays in Criticism*, XXV (1975), p. 310.
22. Jacobus, p. 316.
23. Jacobus, p. 320.
24. Jacobus, p. 324.
25. Gail Cunningham: *The New Woman and the Victorian Novel* (London: Macmillan, 1978), p. 114.
26. John Goode: 'Sue Bridehead and the New Woman' in *Women Writing and Writing about Women*, ed. Mary Jacobus (London: Croom Helm, 1979), pp. 103, 107, 108.
27. Penny Boumelha: *Thomas Hardy and Women* (Brighton: Harvester, 1982), p. 153.
28. Boumelha, p. 150.
29. Rosemarie Morgan: *Women and Sexuality in the Novels of Thomas Hardy* (London and New York: Routledge, 1988), p. 154.
30. Phillip Mallett: 'Sexual Ideology and Narrative Form in *Jude the Obscure*' in *English*, XXXVIII (1989), p. 217.
31. Mallett, p. 222.
32. Mallett, p. 223.
33. Friedrich Nietzsche: *Werke in Drei Banden*, III (München: Hanser, 1960), p. 314. (My translation.)
34. *Jude*, p. 445. (Penguin, p. 429, gives 'however fondly' instead of 'however'.)
35. *Jude*, p. 183 (Penguin, p. 202).
36. *Jude*, p. 282 (Penguin, p. 287).
37. *Jude*, p. 427 (Penguin, p. 413).
38. *Jude*, pp. 337–8 (Penguin, p. 335).
39. *Jude*, p. 280 (Penguin, p. 286).
40. *Jude*, pp. 208, 173 (Penguin, pp. 194, 223).
41. *Jude*, p. 366 (Penguin, p. 360).
42. *Jude*, p. 360 (Penguin, p. 355).
43. *Jude*, p. 346 (Penguin, p. 342).
44. Arnold Kettle: *An Introduction to the English Novel*, Vol. II (London: Hutchinson, 1967), p. 156.

45. Jacobus, p. 320; Widdowson, pp. 223–4.
46. Terence Hawkes: *Structuralism and Semiotics* (London: Methuen, 1977), p. 119.
47. Catherine Belsey: *Critical Practice* (London: Methuen, 1980), pp. 98–102.
48. Jacobus, p. 320.
49. G. K. Chesterton: *The Victorian Age in Literature* (London: Oxford University Press, 1913), p. 143.
50. *Jude*, p. 402 (Penguin, p. 391).
51. *Jude*, pp. 215, 232, 473 (Penguin, pp. 229, 244, 453).
52. *Jude*, p. 145 (Penguin, p. 169).
53. Raymond Williams: *The English Novel from Dickens to Lawrence* (London: Chatto & Windus, 1970), pp. 95–7.
54. *Jude*, p. 411 (Penguin, p. 398); *Romeo and Juliet*, V.i.75.
55. *Jude*, p. 23 (Penguin, p. 64, with 'in the days of the Tower of Babel' instead of 'before the Flood').
56. *Jude*, pp. 137–8 (Penguin, pp. 162–3, with variants).
57. *Jude*, p. 280 (Penguin, p. 286).
58. *Jude*, pp. 260–61 (Penguin, pp. 268–9).
59. *Jude*, p. 143 (Penguin, p. 167). The Greek word τετυφέναι means literally 'to have beaten'.
60. *Jude*, p. 352 (Penguin, p. 348).
61. Eugène Ionesco: *Journal en miettes* (Paris: Mercure de France, 1967), p. 101. (My translation.) A. J. Ayer: *Metaphysics and Common Sense* (London: Macmillan, 1969), p. 205.
62. *Jude*, p. 495 (Penguin, p. 472).

7.2 Bibliography (in chronological order within each section)

TEXTS

Holograph manuscript of *Jude the Obscure*: Fitzwilliam Museum, Cambridge.
Jude the Obscure (London: Osgood, McIlvaine & Co., 1895).
Jude the Obscure (London: Macmillan, 1974).
Jude the Obscure, ed. Norman Page (New York: Norton, 1978).
Jude the Obscure, ed. C. H. Sisson (London: Penguin, 1985).

BIOGRAPHICAL WORKS

Florence Emily Hardy: *The Early Life of Thomas Hardy 1840–1891* (London: Macmillan, 1928).
Florence Emily Hardy: *The Later Years of Thomas Hardy 1892–1928* (London: Macmillan, 1930).

Florence Emily Hardy: *The Life of Thomas Hardy 1840–1928* (London: Macmillan, 1962).

Michael Millgate: *Thomas Hardy: His Career as a Novelist* (London: The Bodley Head, 1971).

The Personal Notebooks of Thomas Hardy, ed. Richard H. Taylor (London: Macmillan, 1978).

Michael Millgate: *Thomas Hardy: A Biography* (Oxford: Oxford University Press, 1982).

Thomas Hardy: *The Life and Work of Thomas Hardy*, ed. Michael Millgate (London: Macmillan, 1985).

The Literary Notebooks of Thomas Hardy, Vol. I, ed. Lennart A. Björk (London: Macmillan, 1985).

CRITICAL, SCHOLARLY AND CONTEXTUAL STUDIES

Mary Ellen Chase: *Thomas Hardy from Serial to Novel* [1927] (New York: Russell & Russell, 1964).

D. H. Lawrence: *Study of Thomas Hardy* in *Phoenix* [Vol. I] (London: Heinemann, 1936).

Albert Guerard: *Thomas Hardy* (Cambridge, Mass.: Harvard University Press, 1949).

J. Hillis Miller: *Thomas Hardy: Distance and Desire* (Cambridge, Mass.: Harvard University Press, 1970).

Thomas Hardy: The Critical Heritage, ed. R. G. Cox (London: Routledge & Kegan Paul, 1970).

Kate Millett: *Sexual Politics* [1970] (London: Virago Press, 1977).

Hardy: The Tragic Novels, ed. R. P. Draper (London: Macmillan, 1975).

Terry Eagleton: *Criticism and Ideology: A Study in Marxist Literary Theory* [1976] (London: Verso, 1978).

Gail Cunningham: *The New Woman and the Victorian Novel* (London: Macmillan, 1978).

John Goode: 'Sue Bridehead and the New Woman' in *Women Writing and Writing about Women*, ed. Mary Jacobus (London: Croom Helm, 1979).

Terry Eagleton: *Walter Benjamin or Towards a Revolutionary Criticism* (London: Verso Editions and NLB, 1981).

David Lodge: Chap. 8 of *Working with Structuralism* (London: Routledge & Kegan Paul, 1982).

Penny Boumelha: *Thomas Hardy and Women: Sexual Ideology and Narrative Form* (Brighton: Harvester, 1982).

Phillip Mallett: 'Woman and Marriage in Victorian Society' in *Marriage and Property*, ed. Elizabeth M. Craik (Aberdeen: Aberdeen University Press, 1984).

George Wotton: *Thomas Hardy: Towards a Materialist Criticism* (Goldenbridge: Gill and Macmillan, 1985).

Critical Studies: Jude the Obscure

Rosemarie Morgan: *Women and Sexuality in the Novels of Thomas Hardy* (London and New York: Routledge, 1988).

Phillip Mallett: 'Sexual Ideology and Narrative Form in *Jude the Obscure*' in *English*, XXXVIII (1989), pp. 211–24.

Peter Widdowson: *Hardy in History: A Study in Literary Sociology* (London and New York: Routledge, 1989).

FOR THE BEST IN PAPERBACKS, LOOK FOR THE

In every corner of the world, on every subject under the sun, Penguin represents quality and variety – the very best in publishing today.

For complete information about books available from Penguin – including Puffins, Penguin Classics and Arkana – and how to order them, write to us at the appropriate address below. Please note that for copyright reasons the selection of books varies from country to country.

In the United Kingdom: Please write to *Dept E.P., Penguin Books Ltd, Harmondsworth, Middlesex, UB7 0DA.*

If you have any difficulty in obtaining a title, please send your order with the correct money, plus ten per cent for postage and packaging, to *PO Box No 11, West Drayton, Middlesex*

In the United States: Please write to *Dept BA, Penguin, 299 Murray Hill Parkway, East Rutherford, New Jersey 07073*

In Canada: Please write to *Penguin Books Canada Ltd, 2801 John Street, Markham, Ontario L3R 1B4*

In Australia: Please write to the *Marketing Department, Penguin Books Australia Ltd, P.O. Box 257, Ringwood, Victoria 3134*

In New Zealand: Please write to the *Marketing Department, Penguin Books (NZ) Ltd, Private Bag, Takapuna, Auckland 9*

In India: Please write to *Penguin Overseas Ltd, 706 Eros Apartments, 56 Nehru Place, New Delhi, 110019*

In the Netherlands: Please write to *Penguin Books Netherlands B.V., Postbus 3507, 1001 AH, Amsterdam*

In West Germany: Please write to *Penguin Books Ltd, Friedrichstrasse 10–12, D–6000 Frankfurt/Main 1*

In Spain: Please write to *Alhambra Longman S.A., Fernandez de la Hoz 9, E–28010 Madrid*

In Italy: Please write to *Penguin Italia s.r.l., Via Como 4, I-20096 Pioltello (Milano)*

In France: Please write to *Penguin Books Ltd, 39 Rue de Montmorency, F-75003 Paris*

In Japan: Please write to *Longman Penguin Japan Co Ltd, Yamaguchi Building, 2–12–9 Kanda Jimbocho, Chiyoda-Ku, Tokyo 101*

FOR THE BEST IN PAPERBACKS, LOOK FOR THE 🐧

PENGUIN CRITICAL STUDIES

Described by *The Times Educational Supplement* as 'admirable' and 'superb', Penguin Critical Studies is a specially developed series of critical essays on the major works of literature for use by students in universities, colleges and schools.

titles published or in preparation include:

SHAKESPEARE
Antony and Cleopatra
As You Like It
Hamlet
Julius Caesar
King Lear
Measure for Measure
A Midsummer Night's Dream
Much Ado About Nothing
Othello
Romeo and Juliet
Shakespeare's History Plays
Shakespeare – Text into Performance
The Tempest
Troilus and Cressida
The Winter's Tale

CHAUCER
Chaucer
The Nun's Priest's Tale
The Pardoner's Tale
The Prologue to the Canterbury Tales